My Time With The Ladies Of Disaster

First Edition

Observations and lessons learned to help build Christian resilience while working for FEMA during and since disaster recovery response for "the Ladies" Katrina, Lee, Rita, Sandy, Wilma, and others. It is incredible what you can observe and learn in hindsight after stressful situations.

This book is to help Christians prepare and prevail through the remainder of these End Times up to the imminent Rapture[1] of Christ's Church. This book may be less useful for those left behind as they face the seven-year Great Tribulation.

Roger Fraumann

This book is dedicated to the memory of Liz, my better half, for 53 years.

Table of Contents

INTRODUCTION

This book is written to help Christians enhance their emergency management knowledge with topics including the incident command system (ICS), three time urgency rules, four response priorities (safety, security, sanitary, and shelter), five disaster management stages, six disaster emotional reaction phases and, most importantly, logistics. Christians need to apply their emergency manager skills while encouraging one another and building resilience in the Christian community.

Remember that about half of all wage earners work for American small businesses, 99% of which have fewer than nine employees. An employer's greatest vulnerability is an interruption to their cash flow, directly impacting their employees, creditors, local economy, and the area's mortgage/rental market. Statistically, about 40 percent of businesses closed by a natural or manufactured disaster never reopen[2], which can, in turn, significantly affect your community's resilience. Small and medium business (SMB) resilience is inseparable from the local community.

Although Satan uses (and or curtails) many electrically enabled technologies through his being the "prince of the power of the air" (Ephesians 2:2[3]), the same technologies are also helpful for facilitating Christian evangelism, particularly in these Last Days.

"In any moment of decision,

the best thing you can do is the <u>right thing</u>,

the next best thing is the <u>wrong thing</u>, and

the worst you can do is <u>nothing</u>.[4]"

THEODORE ROOSEVELT

JOY FIRST

A Christian's response in a disaster is best by focusing on JOY (Jesus, others, and yourself). When working with people who experience difficult situations during a significant disaster, the adage "there are no atheists in foxholes" becomes apparent when so many reach out to God in times of peril. Consider their reaching out as part of your ministry.

Everyone in some way is an emergency manager[5], and may also act as an emergency responder[6] when trained with the necessary skills. In a significant disaster, what we call first responders may very well be second responders or, more accurately, emergency or incident responders as it may take days before any additional assistance can respond. While the emerging aerial drone responder[7] capability may dramatically accelerate the ability to deliver a more rapid response in certain situations, the immediate "feet on the street" continues to have the most significant timely impact.

In preparation to become a good emergency manager, start with your spiritual preparedness and leadership skills[8], then work on your mental, emotional, and physical preparedness. Build your essential knowledge and skills to help your community be resilient. Try to do the greatest good for the greatest number, balanced with the Good Shepherd's parable regarding looking for the proverbial lost sheep. An important first vocabulary lesson when working in a disaster is to consistently be mindful of those who are living as "survivors" and those who died as "dead" or "victims." It is essential to remain clear and concise as possible. Maintaining ambiguity surrounding the certainty of death does not make it any easier.

First, address your "eternal" problem because knowing your own "endgame" gives you the confidence to manage better in an emergency or when confronted by a chaotic situation. As the coming Rapture of the Church is imminent, it is imperative to keep your focus on saving souls before the foretold coming of the Great Tribulation. Failing to be saved beforehand will leave you facing the Great Tribulation and God's wrath on Earth.

Adopting a "2-is-1" mindset for planning and essentials is important, as "1" can quickly become none. If it's critical for you, it's likely critical for others, too. When choosing between similar supplies, choose supplies and tools that lend themselves to multi-purpose use. Many Preppers adopt a bug out (Merriam-Webster 2024)[9] mindset instead of first focusing on personal preparation, knowledge, health, dental care, and fitness. It is useless to commit all your emergency planning towards bugging out only to join a circular firing squad to shoot at the same rabbit. As an aside, if you plan on subsisting only on rabbits, with their near absence of fat, you can end up with protein poisoning.

DISASTERS – CALAMITY OR CHAOS?

Disasters are referred to as calamity when caused by God (Isaiah 45:7[10]), and disasters are referred to as chaos as a result of Satan's deceit and loathing (Isaiah 14:12-17[11]). As God is the creator of all things, it is important to remain calm and overcome times of disaster through patience, kindness, goodness, and faithfulness (Galatians 5:22[12]). While the media may label ongoing demonically inspired chaos as an emergency and crisis, it will be referred to throughout this book as what it is, chaos[13].

While natural calamities continue apace, in these End Times, we also face increasing levels of chaotic and manufactured disasters. The Holy Spirit, working through the New Testament Church, has been restraining much of the flood of evil spirits worldwide. With the reduced restraint because of the growing apostasy of the Church, there is an increasing flood of Satanic chaos[14] (and havoc[15]), which is now beginning to overwhelm the world. In response, we must continue focusing on our eternity while the world increasingly focuses on "Anything But Christ" (ABC). While Christians may gain more confidence knowing their endgame, it may not make it any easier to cope with the growing amount of chaos that seems to surround us.

While knowledge merely provides clarity of truths and facts, it pales to the value of wisdom, which is the proper application of knowledge and practical ability to make consistently good decisions. For example, most cooks know tomatoes are technically a fruit, but they also have the wisdom not to add them to their fruit salad. Since "the fear of the Lord is the beginning of wisdom"(Proverbs 9:10[16]) and "the Lord gives wisdom"(Proverbs 2:6[17]), emergency managers need to keep in mind that any artificial intelligence (AI) derived documents and tools may not have the necessary wisdom to be relied upon when responding to calamity and in particular, chaos. This lack of God's wisdom inherent within AI may form a hidden Achilles' heel in AI-based emergency response tools.

As Dennis Prager writes, "Good intentions without wisdom leads to evil[18]." Even before the advent of AI, the shortage of wisdom in governments was already clearly evident, with five times more people being killed by their government (democide[19]) than killed in all of the wars over the 20th century[20].

LEADERSHIP

At least three key factors affect us personally while living a Christian life through periods of calamity and chaos: **desperation**, **starvation**, and **anarchy**.

- **Desperation** is a psychological loss of hope, reflected by emotional, mental, and behavioral exhaustion. While it may manifest itself during a disaster, as an emergency manager, you must remember that God is our refuge and strength (Psalm 46).

- **Starvation** has a physical impact, affecting your mental clarity and behavior when the body expends more energy than it takes in. An average individual's daily caloric[21] needs may vary between 1,400 and 3,400 calories a day, depending on their level of exertion, sex, and age, and typically are derived from an approximate ratio of 6 grams of protein, 9 grams of carbohydrates and 11 grams of fat, (by weight per 100 calories). Semi-starvation may start when the average person's food intake drops below about 1,600 calories a day[22]. As your caloric intake continues to fall, your symptoms may include irritable mood, fatigue, trouble concentrating, and preoccupation with food thoughts, which may directly impact your ability to perform as an emergency manager.

- **Anarchy** is a political manifestation of failing to enforce the rule of law. Laws protect our general safety and ensure our rights as citizens against abuses by other people, organizations, and the government. The consolidation of power within the government manifests itself as anarchy in various forms, including control over energy, media, resources, weapons, and bioterror. Living in anarchy and without the rule of law (WROL), whether simply because of the absence of law enforcement when the government chooses to ignore the Constitution or when the country loses its sovereignty. A significant opportunity for personal disaster is emerging because any tyrannical government presents the most crucial danger, intending to thrive on desperation, starvation, and the resulting pressure toward population reduction.

While we have enjoyed the Constitutional Blessings of Liberty for the past several hundred years here in America, as the continued attacks on America's Constitution increase and demonic anarchy sets in, there is soon coming a day when our governing laws under the Constitution will become unrecognizable. The challenge for Christians is to continue to follow their duty to resist unlawful commands while remaining subject to moral governing authorities, for example, as underscored by the Nuremberg Trial and the My-Lai courts-martial. The challenge is to stay accountable for non-compliance while enduring increasingly unlawful demands by worldly governments.

According to (Romans 13:1–7)[23], " *Let every person be subject to the governing authorities. For there is no authority except from God, and those that exist have been instituted by God.2 Therefore, whoever resists the authorities resists what God has appointed, and those who resist will incur judgment. 3 For rulers are not a terror to good conduct, but to bad. Would you have no fear of the one who is in authority? Then do what is good, and you will receive his approval, 4 for he is God's servant for your good. But if you do wrong, be afraid, for he does not bear the sword in vain. For he is the servant of God, an avenger who carries out God's wrath on the wrongdoer.5 Therefore, one must be in subjection, not only to avoid God's wrath but also for the sake of conscience. 6 For because of this, you also pay taxes, for the authorities are ministers of God, attending to this very thing. 7 Pay to all what is owed to them: taxes to whom taxes are owed, revenue to whom revenue is owed, respect to whom respect is owed, honor to whom honor is owed.* "

American citizens under the U.S. Constitution are under threat of demonic forces both within the media and various portions of the government striving to ignore the Republic and force a dictatorial democracy[24]. The only legal recourse Christians may soon have is to rely on the Lord's vengeance as stated in Romans 12:19-21[25] " *19 Beloved, never avenge yourselves, but leave it[a] to the wrath of God, for it is written, "Vengeance is mine, I will repay, says the Lord." 20 To the contrary, "if your enemy is hungry, feed him; if he is thirsty, give him something to drink; for by so doing you will heap burning coals on his head." 21 Do not be overcome by evil, but overcome evil with good.* "

As the End Times emerge, a seemingly arbitrary[26] legal enforcement framework will challenge the historic laws assuring the "right of self-defense" in the United States to more fully embrace the growing preparation for the Antichrist. A long time in coming, the CDC's use of the revitalized Creole heritage word "zombie" is now frequently used in disaster scenarios to describe a will-less and speech-less reanimated humanoid that won't shoot back because, as Dave Daigle of the CDC writes, "Zombies don't use guns[27]…" The demonic forces being embraced in government today are working to discourage anything that values human life, in particular, family, self-defense, and the defense of others.

In the United States, case law is rapidly being "matured" to dilute the notions of the castle doctrine and stand-your-ground doctrines[28]. The ongoing domestic government attack on your right of self-defense is constantly using piecemeal semantics attacking "what is yours?", "what is a home?" etc. This process encourages legal obfuscation to erode your confidence and ability to address disaster management issues. It plays towards the constant pressure of an illegitimate government interested in transitioning their citizens towards becoming their subjects. The growing ambiguity related to self-defense is becoming a significant issue of consternation while managing in an emergency.

Moreover, by combining the zombie concept with broken bureaucracy democracy (perhaps more accurately, outright anarchy), we end up with armed bureaucratic clerks mindlessly imposing previously unlawful controls. In a world where guns are nearly ubiquitous, any move to reduce access to guns has the (perhaps intended) consequence of lowering one's ability for self-defense during a disaster. George Tucker wrote in the 1803 *Blackstone's Commentaries regarding the American Second Amendment*[29], "*The right of self-defense is the first law of nature.*" The best way to reduce gun violence is by consistently enforcing existing gun laws[30]. Many mass democides are now accompanied by gun confiscation, with nearly every public mass shooting[31] in the USA since 1990 happening in places where guns were banned. While property owners may declare a gun-free zone for their convenience, they also incur a moral obligation and likely legal liability for duty of care[32]. A disaster will exacerbate the situation even further.

It was a harsh lesson regarding the risk created by the depravity of leadership in New Orleans during Hurricane Katrina when the Mayor and Police Superintendent called for the unlawful confiscation of all guns. It has taken years and lawsuits to start to correct this unconstitutional behavior[33] and coverup. This egregious situation is a classic example of the overreach of government, placing anyone involved in an emergency response in direct danger. At the same time, drug gangs and law enforcement took advantage of the lawless situation, where unscrupulous police were emboldened to go door to door through abandoned homes[34] (under mandatory evacuation), adding to their own personal gun collections. Police and other authorities failing to comply with their oaths under the Constitution demonstrated particularly gross misconduct during a disaster, eroding public confidence at a crucial time during an emergency response.

The growing threat to safety and decline of individual rights is a result of the ongoing community organizer[35] approach towards applying Saul Alinsky's lesson to aggregate power: "They have the guns and therefore we are for peace and for reformation through the ballot. When we have the guns then it will be through the bullet.[36]" The proliferation of gun restriction language now embedded in the numerous state of emergency executive orders is poised to be activated in future "plandemics" and disasters, making it increasingly likely that evil civil servants will opportunistically leverage disasters to seize more unconstitutional power, rendering emergency care increasingly difficult. Intentional chaos will become a commonly used tool, as Saul Alinsky taught, "Never let a crisis go to waste[37]." Christians will become hard-pressed to avoid being drawn into responding to these situations.

EMERGENCY MANAGEMENT PROCESS – USING THE INCIDENT COMMAND STRUCTURE (ICS)

Knowing the established emergency management processes adopted as the Incident Command Structure[38] (ICS) is helpful for an emergency manager. ICS was created during a Southern California Fire Chiefs meeting in 1968 to address the need for a replicable, temporary, scalable multi-agency management structure with common terminology and communications.

Since then, ICS has matured into an all-hazards response process to help optimize the deployment of resources in a standardized hierarchical structure that allows for a coordinated response to organizing activities by multiple agencies both within and outside of government without compromising the decision-making authority of local command. ICS now forms the cornerstone of the National Incident Management System (NIMS) across the United States, and the process is now adopted in many countries.

An ICS-based response is initiated by any experienced person first on the scene, who then becomes the incident commander (typically with budget authority). Then, a capable person should be selected as a scribe as soon as possible. In a larger disaster, it is handy to have a copy of the standardized FEMA ICS forms[39] on hand when possible (such as on a USB thumb drive). Where and when possible, do the greatest good within resource constraints. Establish priorities carefully and consider when and how to perform functions like search and rescue only when needed.

The incident commander is responsible for managing the organization and ensuring safety during the overall emergency response process, including:

1. Maintaining situational awareness[40], including "size up," which typically includes lapping the area,
2. Time management by establishing and maintaining a tempo of operations[41],
3. Factoring in weather and forecasts,
4. Identifying, documenting, and marking hazards and potential mitigation and
5. Maintaining resource awareness, including the need for and supply of personal protective gear and equipment.

On top of everything else, criminals will frequently feel emboldened to commit crimes in disaster areas. Hence, preserving potential crime site evidence and photographs for later legal use is prudent. Using an augmented reality multi-function viewfinder app such as *Theodolite*[42] or a comparable app enables you to capture GPS, time, date, and other information directly on your photographs.

Maintaining total situational awareness skills, reinforced through constant use and training, is vital as it is an essential tool for safe, quick decision-making. As Brandon Webb, former head instructor at the Navy SEAL Sniper School, points out in his book *Total Focus*[43], snipers (and as applied in the case of an emergency manager) must learn to keep aware of the big picture using their reconnaissance and surveillance skills while focusing on target/task at hand. You do this by paying attention to the task's details and developing your skills to keep what you observe in memory while relying on your "mental" peripheral vision.

Emergency response resources are organized into an OPLA-like structure: **operations**, **planning**, **logistics**, and finance/**administration** (alternatively, remember the acronym as OPAL, if it makes it easier to remember):

- **Operations** section may quickly need to use about half the people available while forming into branches, divisions, strike teams, and task forces where appropriate.
- **Planning** section keeps track of resources, situations, de-mobilization, and documentation.
- **Logistics** section organizes services and support, including communications, medical, food, facilities, and supplies.
- **Administration**/finance section tracks all branches' time, costs, and compensation claims.

For example, experienced managers frequently come up with informal situational awareness tools to gauge the impact of a disaster or inclement weather on an affected area, such as what former FEMA Administrator Fugate did with his Waffle House Index[44] by calling potentially affected Waffle House restaurants. A similar "water index" can give one a quick quality-of-life assessment by surveying the availability of potable water, hot water, and safe beverage ice across an affected area (having ice also indicates the availability of electricity).

After leaving FEMA, Mr. Fugate has been building SpotOnResponse[45] to deliver web-based, trusted, crowd-sourced, secure communications and location-based situational awareness leveraging the National Association of Convenience Stores (NACS[46]) and the US Chamber of Commerce Foundation (SABER[47]). As an emergency manager, you may want to maintain a disaster situational awareness big picture by signing up with your local County Office of Emergency Management for updates and alerts, for alerts during disasters in your state at USDHSFEMA[48], and national summaries of FEMA Daily Operations Center briefings from the FEMA National Watch Center at The Disaster Center[49], and a daily Global Disaster Alert and Coordination System newsletter provided by the Joint Initiative of the United Nations and the European Commission at GDACS[50]. While the ICSresponse process was initially created principally for firefighters, it is helpful across a broad range of natural disaster and event responses.

However, imagine you need to respond to a local "active shooter" or armed attack. Two self-organizing rapid response guerrilla tactical models to address modern, potentially lethal, combat human threats are **Swarm** and its cousin, **Stigmergy**.

- Swarm[51] tactic is a four-stage, information-intensive form of tactical maneuver to locate, converge, attack (from two or more directions), and disperse (Swarm LCAD). For example, the military mimicked this behavior by using AI to govern a swarm of drones. This form of tactic is now also applied where the Police are trained to advance towards gunfire.
- Stigmergy[52] is a response tactic borrowed from the swarming-like behavior of ants. It can leverage indirect coordination by using environmental cues to trigger a predetermined rules-based decision-making set of responses for situations without reliable communications (for example, when radio communications are unavailable or unintelligible). For instance, Stigmergy may be used effectively by two or more fighters to confound or even prevail over a superior force by keeping ~100 feet apart while maneuvering to within ~1,000 feet of a potential engagement and, when not engaged, initiating an attack (from two or more directions), and retreating when confronted. This approach may also be helpful for other applications, including conducting searches and rescues in contested areas.

TIME-URGENCY RULE OF 3s

For the emergency manager, time management is essential to managing the overall tempo of operations[53] in a disaster response. It is crucial to manage resources judiciously concerning urgency and goals. A helpful tool to help prioritize and focus is the six Time-urgency Rules of Threes (**SECONDS, MINUTES, HOURS, DAYS, WEEKS,** and **MONTHS**).

THREE SECONDS, SAFETY (including first-aid and security response)
Seconds can make a significant difference, for example, when a victim is bleeding out or the minimal time you have to react during the onset of a home invasion. If you have guns at home, consider keeping them in several smaller gun safes instead of one big safe, particularly in a larger home. Keep several fire extinguishers and first-aid kits[54] in diverse places around the house and your vehicles. Fire extinguishers can also become excellent alternative defensive weapons.

THREE MINUTES, AIR
The average person becomes stressed without being able to take their next breath within three minutes. A typical housefire can consume all the oxygen in a room in three minutes and doubles in size every 30 seconds.

THREE HOURS, SHELTER (including core body temperature)
The urgency of the need for shelter can depend on several factors, including weather and the survivor's clothing. The primary concern is the potential for hypothermia, particularly in older adults, babies, and those using medication. Hypothermia is a medical emergency when the body loses heat faster than it can produce. Even a seemingly mild temperature of 65 °F must be considered potentially life-threatening, particularly if the survivor is chilled from rain, sweat, or cold water.

THREE DAYS, POTABLE WATER (including prescription medicines)
Typically, search and rescue operations start reaching a dehydration threshold, where survivors can begin turning into victims after three days due to lack of water. Depending upon the circumstances, the emergency response process may start transitioning from response into recovery. An emergency manager is also responsible for safety during the disaster response, including ensuring adequate hydration for the responders. Obtaining and maintaining about a gallon of potable water daily per person, including all survivors who have remained in the affected area, is imperative. It is easy to be distracted by all the demands of emergency management and not notice your own less frequent or dark urination, so it is essential to maintain situational awareness. If you do not keep drinking enough liquids, you can start experiencing confusion, dizziness, fatigue, and start making mistakes.

The simultaneous loss of both the Internet and GPS[55] for time synchronization will create an existential threat to the modern economy of the United States within three days. If GPS[56] time synchronization signals are unavailable, transportation-related digital communication links and other applications such as telecommunications, banking, commerce, and the Internet will be severely impacted. It is "estimated that the combined loss of GPS position, navigation, and timing (PNT) services would damage the U. S. economy by at least $1 billion per day.[57]"

Considering over a third of the American population is pre-diabetic or diabetic. A quarter are taking four or more prescription drugs, and arranging access to medical care and pharmaceutical services after a disaster may become essential within three days.

THREE WEEKS, FOOD

In the 1940s, Mahatma Gandhi stopped eating and only drank sips of water for 21 days during his hunger strike, demonstrating that under exceptional circumstances, someone can live for up to three weeks without food as long as they have water to drink. When you stop eating, your body starts to break down its tissues for food, potentially disrupting all the vital processes of your systems. In short, what we eat is central to maintaining our health. If we go without eating, we start to experience hunger, irritability, the ability to focus, and loss of productivity.

While some use intermittent fasting to improve health, occasionally not eating for up to three days (while maintaining adequate hydration) may trigger beneficial autophagy (self-eating) of poorly functioning cells, improved muscle mass, and immune function. More extended fasting periods may increase the risk of symptoms, including a lack of energy, bloating, constipation, dehydration, drop in blood sugar levels, fainting, fatigue, headaches, insomnia, mood changes, nausea, trouble concentrating, vomiting, and eventually, death. Something for a Christian to keep in mind is that in these later days, the growing use of the word "famine" in the Church increasingly refers to the lack of hearing the words of the Lord (Amos 8:11[58]).

THREE MONTHS, COMMUNITY (Some may say three YEARS)

An effective emergency manager must strive to associate with those who share trust, values, and loyalty. Good neighbors willing to share knowledge, experience, and skills are invaluable. Everyone needs meaningful work, even if they can only stand as fireguards late at night because even the community's most capable Rambo needs to sleep.

FOUR RESPONSE PRIORITIES

An emergency manager is well served to adopt an "Occam's razor[59]" style decision process, which works towards enabling better decision-making by choosing the more straightforward choice and keeping your decision-making as simple as possible by following the "KISS principle[60]" ("Keep It Super Simple").

In particular, when a manager sets priorities with a sense of urgency, it may be best to frame the decision with the irrefutable facts of how it was arrived at. And, if time permits, relay the reasoning to any surrounding responders, which blunts second-guessing. Where resources may not be divisible, or when you find yourself negotiating for others, such as for fire or flood control, food for your family's survival, or even rescue or hostage negotiation, you may find "splitting the difference" is not an option. An excellent book on negotiation is *Never Split The Difference*[61] (Raz 2016) by former FBI hostage negotiator, Chris Voss.

Practice using "two ears, one mouth," and remember how much more you can learn with your mouth shut. Control your "command" voice and exude confidence because lives may depend on it. Take notes, or if possible, have a scribe. It may be forgotten if not written down, so try to capture the details, particularly numbers.

When faced with many complex challenges in an emergency, try sequentially prioritizing your disaster response by filtering them through the Response Priority Rule of the Four S's: safety, security, sanitary, and shelter:

SAFETY IS THE FIRST RESPONSE PRIORITY

Safety takes precedence because it serves as a foundation for the others. Without safety first, your security, sanitation, and shelter plans quickly fall at risk, especially when working with others. For example, if you don't ensure safety first, your security measures could be easily breached, sanitary conditions deteriorate and compound the situation, and shelter may not provide adequate protection. Safety is a fundamental pillar by which the other response priorities remain relevant.

Remember that those who may be at the most significant risk are those you don't see. For example, those with disabilities in an affected community are two to four times[62] more likely to die or be critically injured, and seniors over 60 years old are at greater risk. Over 70% of those[63] who died in Hurricane Katrina were seniors.

SAFETY CONSIDERATIONS

As an emergency manager, setting an example by prioritizing safety becomes contagious. Flag or mark, make a list, and prudently avoid hazards or situations until you are ready to address them. Identify and appropriately utilize people with medical, HazMat, and other specialized training and skills. Without proper treatment and medication, the greatest threat during disaster recovery is from disease and infection. For example, during the Civil War, for every three who died during combat, five died of disease. Complement your first-aid training by maintaining at least two first-aid/trauma medical kits[64] and fire extinguishers, with at least one in your home and one in your car. If you have the resources and training, keep an oxygen generator or oxygen bottles and a 365-day supply of essential medications on hand[65].

Learning first-aid basics is a good start towards becoming a competent emergency manager. Consider completing Red Cross Training[66] and maintaining certifications for at least the first four courses, including first aid, cardiopulmonary resuscitation (CPR), automated external defibrillator (AED), and basic life support (BLS), as an excellent start towards building competence as an emergency manager, including:

- First aid (in particular when using ABCDE[67] and MARCH[68])
  Clinical-oriented (airway, breathing, circulation, disability, exposure) and
  Trauma-oriented (massive bleeding, airway, respiration, circulation, hypothermia)
- Cardiopulmonary resuscitation (CPR)
- Automated external defibrillator (AED)
- Basic life support (BLS)
- Advanced life support (ALS)
- Pediatric advanced life support (PALS)
- Certified nursing assistant (CNA)
- Swimming and water safety
- Lifeguarding

For those who have the time and resources, volunteering to be part of your local Red Cross Disaster Action Team (DAT[69]) is a great way to become trained and a part of your community's emergency response capability.

Another excellent volunteering opportunity is in those communities that have an active local Community Emergency Response Team (CERT[70]). CERT is typically associated with the local Fire Department. If your community does not yet have a CERT, build one while helping build on your emergency manager skills. The CERT training[71] includes:

- CERT ICS operations, planning, logistics, and administration (OPLA)
- ICS (including operations management and tempo of operations)
- Standardized Incident Command System
- Safety, security, sanitary and shelter
- Fire safety (including size up, extinguisher use, hazards)
- How to turn off (and flag) the utilities
- Medical triage and treatment (clinical and trauma)
- Search and rescue operations (including cribbing)
- Disaster preparedness, mitigation, and psychology

An example of a CERT Team success was during Hurricane Wilma when the trunked-radio system failed in Collier County, FL. The Waterways/Big Corkscrew Island Fire & Rescue District (BCIFR) CERT completed their Preliminary Damage Assessment (PDA) in less than an hour[72], covering 823 homes across a completely isolated four-square-mile area, and then communicated the results to the BCIFR Emergency Operations Center (EOC) via amateur radio. Another outstanding example of a community CERT is Bainbridge Prepares[73], which has been building extensive community resilience for over 12 years.

Those seeking hands-on experience volunteering with a relief organization can subscribe to the FEMA Voluntary Organization Information Sharing and Engagement (VOISE[74]) to learn more.

SECURITY IS THE SECOND RESPONSE PRIORITY

It is essential to build relationships actively for security and effective management. Emergency managers have traditionally had a closer relationship with the Fire Department and need to consciously reach out and build working relationships with other organizations, including law enforcement, health services, local governments, and logistics supply chains. Emergency managers work with a very diverse group of police, firefighters, and healthcare workers, who all tend to have high integrity, be extraverted, very conscientious, and have high social responsibility. Their perceived pressure is typically on getting things done right the first time. As an emergency manager, it is imperative to respect that.

Emergency management should look beyond ensuring the physical safety of emergency responders and stakeholders and also address the need for security and continuity of operations for the operational survival of local jurisdictions, businesses, and nongovernmental organizations (NGOs).

In particular, local governments and neighborhoods need to practice the lessons from the broken windows theory[75] to quickly repair or remove physical signs of disorder and incivility within a community. A broken window, left unrepaired, invites further breaking of windows, contributing to subsequent occurrences of serious crime and a generally degraded quality of life.

For the emergency manager, at least four forces are compounding the difficulty of recovery from a disaster and contributing towards an environment conducive to chaos, including an unelected deep state (running a double government[76] through deception), the unaccountable globalist "elite" class[77], and the two major communist powers including the Maoist CCP of China[78] and the Stalinist Putin's Russia[79]. All four forces share chaotic coopetition agendas, favoring a one-world-oriented form of government and all opposing the God of the Universe.

It is remarkable how many Elites (and others) appear to subscribe to the theory that humans are a blight on the Earth. One only needs to search the Internet with phrases like "elite population control[80]" to gain insight into the degree of fact-checking deceit and a cause for concern about the seriousness of the unfolding consequences of the restraint of power being imposed on the lower and middle classes and the subsequent resulting pressure towards democide.

Throughout the 20th century, China is second only to Russia for deaths by democide[81]. And now, two Chinese Colonels assert in their update of Sun Tzu called *Unrestricted Warfare*[82] (1999), the prevailing trend of moving to "kinder weapons," which, in their view, underscores the need to move beyond the antiquated "Mutual assured destruction" (MAD) mindset with its 1,000 times over-kill, towards a more efficient "one shot, one kill" approach and ultimately achieving victory by not needing to kill at all, overtly, but simply gaining control through compulsion. In reality, the end of MAD came about because of the proliferation of asymmetrical warfare, in particular, where there is an open willingness to martyr entire populations for an ideology.

An example of starvation being willfully used to create a disaster was Stalin ordering a manufactured famine to murder nearly 4 million in 1932-34 in Ukraine called the "Holodomor[83]". Russia has long exercised warfare and democide as reliable instruments of national power[84]. Even Pol-Pot (a Russian Stalinist Comintern[85]) saved bullets by killing millions in Cambodia, including by inflicting hypoxia using blue plastic bags in the late 1970s.

Today, the highway to a democide Hell is being paved with good intentions, including the increasing vocal demand for the right of assisted suicide[86]" (euthanasia[87]) starting to drown out the right of self-defense. These growing influences run counter to effective disaster recovery and stress the importance of personal emergency management in uncertain times.

SECURITY – PLAN AHEAD

Plan ahead and avoid reactionary "running" with the herd. Of the four levels of Cooper's color code situational awareness (white, yellow, orange, and red), it is best to maintain a condition yellow[88], which is remaining generally relaxed but keeping aware of who and what is going on around you.

Maintaining preparedness is vital[89] before any sign of pending disaster. The easiest way to address any potential need to bug out is focusing on God's Will. If possible, an ideal worldly preparedness posture is to focus on at least five things:
1. pay all taxes,
2. be able to feed your family and have access to potable water,
3. medical, dental, and mental health,
4. own land, your house, or at least a tent, and
5. maintain little to no debt and other external obligations.

It is an essential emergency management practice always to be planning and building worthwhile relationships. Also, when and where possible, develop and maintain a mental list of hazards, vulnerable people, potential staff position candidates, and a pre-identified pool of qualified, trained staff and allies ready to deploy. Simply put, relationships are key, and truth and trust are essential qualities that can never be assumed. It is hard to maintain trust, particularly when the "facts" historically may have been abused. Knowing who you can trust is critically important when making a bug in[90] vs. bug out or co-sheltering decision. For example, a fair test of your level of trust is your confidence while trading ammunition, sharing a knife or other limited supplies within your community, and avoiding arming a potential adversary.

Managing volunteers has unique challenges; vouching for and checking individual qualifications and credentials is essential. A simple indicator of the level of public trust that may be established is if the individual can provide teacher or bank teller credentials. Additionally, concealed carry permit holders, commercial driver's licenses (CDL), pilot credentials, and even an amateur radio license can give one an insight into building trust. Additional issues to consider include exposing yourself to personal liability or incurring potential workers' compensation and resource liability for any employer, government body, or NGO you may find yourself representing. Consider the significant differences in how various states address volunteer workers' compensation coverage. For example, when volunteering for a sandbagging detail, who might be sued if someone hurts themselves?

Non-governmental organizations (NGOs), including The Salvation Army[91], American Red Cross[92], Habitat for Humanity[93], or veteran-led Rubicon[94], may help you address unmet needs. At the same time, locally organized houses of worship may step forward to help address sheltering w/pet care, special needs, and elderly care. Even sandbagging or childcare sharing requires planning, safety, and coordination. In contrast, unvetted and untrained spontaneous volunteers might become a liability management headache and cause more harm than good.

Examples of failing to vet volunteers properly include:

- As a FEMA Disaster Recovery Center (DRC[95]) was being established at a particularly challenging time in Florida shortly after a hurricane, a person claiming to be the local Mayor arrived, quickly ingratiated himself with the State and Federal resources and assisted with facilitating local recovery efforts. After a while, he was discovered not to be the elected Mayor but rather the local town's highly knowledgeable and friendly drunk.
- Another example occurred during the Witch wildfire in Southern California, where over a half-million people were under mandatory evacuation. One of the evacuation shelters was established at the Qualcomm Football Stadium. A childcare area was spontaneously created by mutually collaborating parents who shared resources to watch for each other's children, where it was subsequently later discovered that one of the "spontaneous volunteers" was a convicted child molester.

There are various sources where you can learn more about determining who you can trust, including Paul Ekman's book *Unmasking the Face*[96]" and Marty Nemko's article *How Can You Tell Who to Trust?*[97].

SECURITY – PNT (POSITIONING, NAVIGATION, AND TIMING)

Running from a disaster may place you in greater danger unless you have a plan, resources, and purpose. Accurately determining the time and navigating to or from various locations is essential during a crisis. Maintaining communications without accurate time and mapping makes success highly problematic. A great way to build your navigation skills is to participate in a growing sport called orienteering[98].

Today, positioning, navigation, and timing (PNT[99]) supports the continued functioning of critical infrastructure and recovery efforts. Accurate time coordination is essential to maintain a consistent tempo of operations and manage accurate locational awareness in a disaster. Alternatives[100] to PNT are roughly equivalent to the functions provided by the modern U.S. Global Positioning System (GPS) satellite constellation and include relative navigation system, Inertial Navigation System (INS), absolute navigation by celestial navigation and even bathymetric navigation when in a submarine.

Nearly every electronic financial transaction, including ATMs, credit card transactions, and cash registers, depends on accurate time signals from NIST[101] Internet time service via either Internet (ITS[102]) or satellite-derived time service through the GPS (GPS[103]). Hence, access to and reliability in the Internet and GPS for accurate time has become essential for the modern economy.

While ancients used various forms of celestial, terrestrial, and magnetic navigation, few of us would want to or are capable of, depending on using the Polaris star or compass for navigating in the modern world. Most civilian navigation is made easy using GPS, which relies on a polyconic latitude/longitude (Lat/Long[104]) coordinate system commonly used with aviation, maritime[105], and consumer units today. The dangers are the abuse and vulnerabilities[106] of the GPS, which may render the system untrustworthy when it is most depended upon.

For example, after a disaster destroyed all area road signs and the area's cellular phone service, the author found that a Garmin automotive GPS unit made a significant difference in finding the initial local disaster recovery locations. The internal one-hour battery also enabled handheld use, which enabled an efficient preliminary damage assessment and reestablishing community relations.

During World War II, the Russians developed an orthomorphic six-degree Universal Traverse Mercator (UTM[107]) coordinate grid system system to enable easier map coordination for their artillery. Today, America's military uses a global UTM coordinate system called the Military Grid Reference System (MGRS[108]). FEMA and public safety services use a simplified U.S. domestic version called the U.S. National Grid (USNG[109]). MGRS/USNG, with its "easting" and "northing," appears to be more complex as compared with lat/long and even simple GPS, which can be measured in minutes/seconds or decimals, and USNG can be very confusing to the uninitiated during the stress of a disaster.

Any technological risk needs to be factored in before depending on it for accurate navigation in times of crisis. Compounding the problem is the currently highly pervasive dependence by commercial, financial, transportation, and communications systems on the precise time signals delivered by the vulnerable GPS satellite system. As various navigation technologies have matured through the ages, we have moved from visual observation & memory through dead reckoning (i.e., using waypoints), celestial, radio navigation (i.e., ground-based Loran and instrument navigation), satellite GPS, to various forms of increasingly sophisticated inertial navigation (including the now emerging quantum gyroscope). The world of PNT will change radically with the forthcoming creation and adoption of quantum systems capable of atomic-level accuracy.

Meanwhile, knowing the time and keeping track of the days on a calendar may become critically important in a grid-down situation. Even an accurate working timepiece can make a significant difference if there is a long-term grid-down event. For example, a proven, reliable mechanical wind-up watch like a Hamilton khaki field mechanical (MIL-W-46374B[110] or MIL-W-3818[111] (military spec watch). Or, for those well-heeled, a manual winding Omega Speedmaster Moonwatch[112] (the only chronometer qualified for NASA EVA and moonshots) is so reliable and accurate that it could easily be adapted to be used as a local time standard in support of an isolated recovery operation. Unless the local town church bell can give you an accurate relative time hack, you may want to be able to tune in to 5 or 10 MHz[113] for an audio WWV[114] radio time signal. Or, you may want to use an extremely accurate and convenient wall clock using NIST WWVB[115] synchronized time signals, such as a La Crosse Technology UltrAtomic Wall Clock[116].

Anytime you want to write down the day and time consistently, use the standardized ISO 8601[117] extended date/time format (EDTF) standard. You write year-month-day using a hyphen between calendar components and a colon between clock components (e.g., 2005-09-24 10:00:00). Consistently using a standard method of date and time notation enables accurate and consistent annotation for historical events and future planning.

Having maps marked in one or more of these commonly used coordinate systems is beneficial. When purchasing maps, look for maps accurately marked with UTM and lat/long grid coordinates, such as USGS maps[118]. If you know how to use easting and northing and have a UTM grid reader[119], you are a step ahead in accurately locating specific points on a map without GPS.

Consider what you need if you are in a grid-down situation. Valuable types of paper maps to have on hand include:
- Road maps (determine which County map to standardize by asking your local Sheriff which paper map they keep for emergency use in their patrol car). Also, keep a Rand McNally large-scale road atlas[120] in the car.
- Topographical/reconnaissance[121] (geological survey) maps

- Fish and game resource maps
- SpiderWeb[122] contingency planning (for evacuation contingency planning) or FEMA Guide to Urban Evacuation mapping[123]
- Trail/hiking maps
- Railroad/pipeline[124] maps
- Historical maps
- Radiological event evacuation[125] mapping
- List/map of prearranged emergency meeting locations for family and friends.

SECURITY – SITUATIONAL AWARENESS

Maintaining situational awareness is essential to knowing your neighbors because your community's safety and security are critical to your home's safety and security. Knowing like-minded neighbors and building a network with those interested in sharing their essential skills and services is important. As an emergency manager, always understand what opposes your Christian walk with the Lord (1 John 2:26-29[126]). Maintaining situational awareness[127] is critical for safe and effective decision-making. It involves staying aware of what is happening around you and considering all factors appropriately.

Avoid idleness, which can become contagious and lead to potentially deadly lethargy, particularly at a moment when rapid action may be needed most. Avoid conspicuous consumption, which has the potential of attracting undesirable burdens. Avoid tactical behavior and clothing, work to be invisible by maintaining a neutral demeanor vocabulary, and have no memorable smell. J.J. Luna's book *How to Be Invisible*[128], Third Edition, is an excellent read on the topic. In particular, dressing or acting "tactically" may put people on edge, make you memorable, and trigger a scan for weapons.

SECURITY – COMMUNITY DEFENSE

The security of your home is dependent on the security of your neighborhood. One of the advantages of remaining in your home is maintaining access to your pre-existing logistical supply and tools that you may already have. You don't have to build new relationships and are not being forced to start from scratch, determining who you can trust and may have to barter with. Consider barter a critical skill because even the wealthy will gladly exchange all sorts of things for more time. Adopt a barter mindset[129] where knowledge, access to information, mending materials, shoes, knives, binoculars, water purifiers, alcohol, canned/dried foods, medicines, voltage protectors, hygiene products, flashlights, batteries, candles, matches, coffee, smoking materials, fuel, vehicle parts, and skills with first aid/medical/dental, cooking, farming, animal husbandry, food preservation, and blacksmithing all have value

Nothing is worse in an emergency than being trapped in an apathetic community. If you find yourself in one, work beforehand to become part of the solution by contacting local law enforcement and finding or forming[130] a Neighborhood Watch team[131]. Competence with quality skills and trust built over time builds community.

Encourage neighbors to keep an eye out for each other's homes. For example, you can communicate without opening the door using inexpensive FRS walkie-talkies for neighborhood comms. Greywolf Survival's article on *Neighborhood Watch*[132] and the CDM *Neighborhood Protection Plan*[133] provides excellent insights into finding like-minded people in your neighborhood. Another way is to become active with the security team of your local house of worship or form/join a County Home Guard to support your Sheriff (particularly an elected Constitutional Sheriff[134]). In particular, you need to find a way to help your Sheriff (and, by extension, all first responders, food producers, and their families) so they can continue to operate through periods of grid-down or unrest.

Assume nothing, and be vigilant for your safety. Trust cannot be assumed. Knowing who you can trust should be a significant consideration when making a bug in versus bug out decision. One of the benefits of bugging in is maintaining a better understanding concerning the castle doctrine and the increasingly legislated but ambiguous duty to retreat legal posturing, particularly when it is very early in the morning in your residence.

Being able to protect your unambiguous right of self-defense for your family, particularly when in transit or housed in a weapon-restricted shelter, can significantly reduce your options for safety. If temporary evacuation is necessary, attempt to co-evacuate (and co-shelter, where possible) people with their animals, including household pets. Service and assistance animals will improve your ability to anticipate and comply with evacuation orders and your chances for a safe return.

When possible, pre-determine the best rooms in your home and your place of business to be your safe room[135]. Some people may also view their safe room as a storm shelter). An excellent guide for a proper safe room is the FEMA safe room[136] page, typically the building's most structurally and physically secure potential sanctuary point.

SECURITY – HOME DEFENSE
Implement a multi-layer defense-in-depth approach for home defense, including deterrence, fortification, warning, confrontation, EmComm[137].

Deterrence
Have solar-powered motion-activated lighting on all approaches to your home. Have obvious video cameras (and make sure they have sufficient capability for identification and recognition[138]). Use critter deterrent strips[139] on fence tops, etc. Install bollards[140], boulders, and moats. Use plants[141] strategically, and consider plants such as multiflora rose (beware, some think it is an invasive species, while others believe it is a "living fence").

Fortification
Install deadbolt locks with 3" attachment screws on all exterior doors. Install bars[142], bollards, door armor[143], window armor (such as 3M Safety Film[144]), door wedges, garage door bracing[145], and consider metal roofing to impede arson.

Alarms
Home alarms (such as SimpliSafe[146] to ADT[147]), intrusion detection and trip wires[148] (which can be as simple as a fish line across your yard with empty soup cans holding a few bolts to rattle), a dog (even a tiny yapping dog eliminates the element of surprise), and gravel around the home which can make noise, are all effective.

Confrontation
A fire extinguisher (such as a 5-pound ABC dry chemical hanging on the wall by each outside door), knowing Krav Maga[149] martial arts, or having a survival axe[150], tomahawk, machete, Rapier sword, squirt gun with bleach/muriatic acid, tactical pen, box cutter, sword, spear, bow and arrow, and

non-lethal weapons (including pepper/bear spray, mace spray (phenacyl chloride), stun gun/Taser, cane, baseball bat, blackjack, or even just having a simple Super Soaker of unpleasantness or soapy detergent can make a difference.

EmComm (emergency communications) and data planning must use communications mediums that are not reliant on infrastructure. Communications planning is critical to situational awareness, initiating and coordinating responses, and periodic situation reports (SITREP) and should be included in any applicable family communications planning[151].

Maintain a cyber go-bag containing digital pictures for identification and PDFs of your tax records, insurance, accounts/passwords, driver's licenses, passports, health/shot records, etc. This can be as simple as an encrypted folder on a USB memory stick with a redundant backup on a shared drive and as a fallback in the cloud.

It is also essential to have physical evacuation plans for travel to pre-determined multiple rally points outside the building, starting within your neighborhood, then outside the city and further out in another state. If you become separated, plan to leave a physical note or flag at each site so as you move further to the following site, others can readily see that you have already been there. Share a trusted mutual contact point in another state with whom you can communicate and mutually share your status and plans.

SANITARY IS THE THIRD RESPONSE PRIORITY

A cascade of failures in a severe supply chain disruption will likely impact diesel fuel, gasoline, propane, heating fuel, food, medicines, and more. Any combination of these supply chain disruptions will place a significant demand for emergency management and the need for preparation.

A modern home has five complementary systems that work well together but are all technology and energy dependent. These systems include: 1. electrical, 2. plumbing/sewer, 3. heating ventilation, 4. cooling (HVAC), and 5. waste removal:

ELECTRICAL

Electricity is the crucial enabler of keeping modern life sanitary. If reliable delivery of electricity becomes unavailable, it will present significant challenges for maintaining any semblance of a contemporary quality of life.

Modern homes in America have standardized on 240 volt 60 cycle (Hertz) alternating current (AC), which is delivered from two "poles" (or each end) of a distribution transformer with the center "tap" of the windings grounded and treated as a neutral (which is also bonded to Ground). In this way, the two poles provide a potential of 240 volts, while each pole's to neutral potential is 120 volts. The reliable (uninterrupted) electricity supply makes things like refrigeration and elevators practical. Only through abundant energy can we depend on electricity for more than lighting, including cooking, heating/air conditioning, computer/communications, and entertainment. From a resilience standpoint, it would be wise to consider your dependence on electricity's continuing availability and reliability before buying anything that plugs into the wall.

The availability of light-emitting diodes (LED), which consume less than a third of the electrical power versus an incandescent light bulb makes it much easier to fall back on battery (or solar-recharged battery power) to provide lighting when the utility power is off. However, a grid-down event may significantly reduce outdoor and security lighting. Lighting workarounds, including candles[152] (depending, roughly 1 hour per inch), oil lamps[153] (approximately 5 hours a day for two months per gallon), and an innovative gravity-powered NowLight gravity light[154] from Africa is slowly improving in quality and is something you may want to consider in future preparation planning.

As maintaining reliable power for refrigeration becomes much more problematic, keep an ice cube or two in a readily visible zip-lock bag in the freezer as a straightforward method of monitoring and determining whether the freezer has temporarily lost power long enough to unthaw (hence, your food may be spoiled but has subsequently refrozen). This can help reduce the risk of unintentional food poisoning from an unobserved power outage.

Unless you live where it never thaws and can store your frozen food outdoors or already have a sizeable solar generator[155] (with sufficient battery and charge to keep working through the night), you will likely need to use a fuel-powered generator. Fossil fuel-powered generators may be helpful in short-term power interruptions. However, a long-term grid-down event may necessitate alternative food storage solutions like root cellars.[156] Planning to have an off-grid solar-powered refrigeration unit[157] may also form part of a solution. Suppose your goal is to be able to keep your refrigerator freezer food frozen using a gas-powered generator while the electrical power is off for a week and it is warm outside. Assuming your portable generator consumes 3/4trs of a gallon of gasoline per hour, and you need to run it an hour four times a day, you will likely need at least 21 gallons of gas on hand for the week.

In the meantime, you may want to be able to can your meat quickly to preserve it before it spoils. Canning seems a misnomer because you will likely use pint and quart glass jars with specialized one-time use or reusable sealing lids, such as Tatler[158]. There are two canning methods for preserving food: a pressure cooker[159] or a water bath[160]. It is wise to use the pressure cooker method when canning anything containing low-acid foods, including fish, meat, poultry, seafood, and vegetables. A highly recommended book is *The Homestead Canning Cookbook* (G. Varozza 2019) by Georgia Varozza.

A widespread power outage can rapidly lead to the need for frozen food consolidation across the neighborhood and coordinated fuel conservation unless the fuel stations in your area are somehow unaffected. Even if you were to go to a gas station and offer to use your generator to power a gas pump, there is no easy way to connect. Fuel stations need to have a shore power[161] connection capability to connect to a generator and pump fuel safely when the grid is down. However, the EPA regulators seem to have ignored national resilience as a critical requirement.

Fans provide air circulation and assist with air filtration. If your ambient temperature is below 95 °F[162], air circulation may help maintain comfort through evaporation. However, if the ambient temperature exceeds 95 °F, cooling effectiveness is reduced under certain conditions (such as your skin's continued ability to sweat.) Using a rechargeable 12VDC battery-operated fan may improve quality of life considerably. A bucket-top misting fan[163] can be helpful as a battery-operated evaporative cooler in drier climate areas.

Those with carpeting will find vacuuming problematic without electrical power. You may want to factor in the ease of sanitation and how to clean your floor without electricity when you select a flooring type.

Power distribution in the home of the future[164] may eventually become primarily DC. In the meantime, you should effectively plan toward implementing a microgrid[165] in your home by using solar panels, batteries, appliances, and other devices to make your home significantly more resilient. In the short term, it may be prudent to standardize using 12VDC as your standard DC supply voltage. Your automobile could act as a mobile generator plant in an emergency, with 5VDC commonly being used with the USB-A/USB-C standard connector (think cell phone, iPad, etc.). Rotating a supply of smaller cell batteries[166] ranging from 3VDC CR2032 (watch batteries) and an assortment of 1.5V AAA, AA, C, and D rechargeable batteries may be useful. However, battery technology is constantly changing, and emerging solid-state battery technology[167] will likely revolutionize your energy storage within the next decade.

Consider the energy requirements when buying devices, adapters, converters, and chargers to/from and between these voltages to help you better prepare for power interruptions. Portable solar and crank generators capable of charging these various voltages will become invaluable. Many interests compete to make a new household wiring standard, either at 48VDC or whether to go higher. Wiring expense becomes a significant part of your overall cost, and the higher DC voltages can halve (or more) your installation costs. Broadly adopting Power over Ethernet (POE)[168] may solve low-voltage DC distribution wiring needs. Consider how Cat 5/CAT6a[169] wiring is already used to replace a home's formerly pervasive 4-wire-telephone wiring.

While pumps, other motor-driven devices, and induction heating for the time being will likely remain dependent on the high-voltage AC commercial power grid, a growing DC Standard for the home may very well migrate to 48 VDC POE and use DC-to-DC converters/solid-state transformers (SST[170]) to supply other needed voltages (at relatively low current) closer to each point of consumption. Generally, The National Electric Code (NEC[171]) 70E Article 720 and other requirements focus on AC and DC circuit's potential risk to life when operating voltages exceed 50 volts. It is easy for amateur electricians to make mistakes that can become fatal, like connecting multiple solar panels in series, without consulting the NEC code book. It only takes three panels in series to exceed 50 volts (open circuit). Still, balancing the risks and rewards with ease and safety of use with voltages under 50 volts is helpful. Virtually no circuits over 50 volts should use any wiring under 12 AWG (copper or the equivalent larger AWG in aluminum) other than for lighting. Circuits supplying more than one appliance must start with 10 AWG (copper or the equivalent larger AWG in aluminum).

WATER

Ensure your water heater is physically secured in case of seismic disturbance, which can be installed easily using a water heater seismic strap[172]. You don't need to be in a known earthquake zone to add the extra precaution. In the event of supply chain interruptions, water supply pressure interruption will likely result in most municipal water supply systems, with the water becoming non-potable (unsuitable for drinking) and then necessitating boil orders or other water filtration before it can be used for safe drinking. Bathing and showering will become problematical without pressurized running water. Even simple things, like rinsing your toothbrush with non-potable water, can kill you.

Installing a UV-light filtration enabled reverse osmosis water filtration system will help protect your icemaker from making ice with non-potable water in the event of water pressure fluctuation, for example, an APEC roes-phuv75[173]. Be careful, however, as the resulting reverse osmosis (RO) water contains no minerals, so it is not useful for household plants and hydroponic systems.

Maintaining a potable water supply in communities of over 3,300 people presents many issues, most of which fall under the America's Water Infrastructure Act (AWIA[174]). Optimistically, many larger water districts anticipate eventually having low-energy nuclear reactor (LENR[175]) microgrid-based solutions coming to the rescue. Maintaining a potable water supply in small towns, rural areas, and farms is essential, as this is where most of the nation's food comes from. It's one thing to draw from a surface pond to fill a watering trough. It is something else entirely to maintain the capability to draw from a deep well and then store and deliver the potable water under pressure. An example of a solar solution is RPS Solar Pumps[176]. Key issues involve knowing your solar zone, primary water use, daily gallons, well depth in vertical feet, and whether an elevated gravity tank is (or could be) available. In the meantime, many farmers and ranchers rely on their tractors' power-take-off (PTO) capability (roughly 1Kw per 2HP[177]). Still, it is a valid solution as long as the diesel fuel supply lasts.

Additional options may include adding a hand pump capability to your existing water well (up to 325 feet deep) using technology such as a Simple Pump[178]. Alternatively, in locations with a high-water table and sandy soil, consider possibly driving a new 25-foot deep "shallow well," "driven point well," or "sand well" using technology such as from Water Source[179].

GRAY WATER

It is prudent to plan to be able to conserve and reuse water safely in case your water supply becomes interrupted or limited. Just because your lightly used water may no longer be potable[180] (suitable for drinking), many forms of gray water[181] sources, such as capturing your used water from your sink, shower, and washing machine, may be ideal to then use for other purposes including flushing down a toilet (which in this context subsequently becomes black water[182]). Preparing to do gray water recovery, storage, and transfer requires planning to have several holding tubs ready for water, as well as hoses and pumps to implement your various water transfer methods and contingencies.

Without pre-planning, accomplishing laundry without a reliable power and water supply becomes problematic. For example, a typical washing machine load uses between 7 and 20 gallons of water (weighing between ~60-160 pounds) per wash load. For example, prepare for water recovery and repurposing using one or more wheeled ~25-gallon tanks (each weighing well over 200 pounds when full.) Planning for a workable indoor or outdoor clothesline/drying solution and cloths-pins will also become essential. Alternatively, consider moving closer to a stream and a big rock;').

Potable water and edible food are challenging to keep sanitary and are essential for life. It is critical to prevent contamination because it becomes difficult, if not impossible, to recover after accidental contamination. Infection was the number one killer during the Civil War and was frequently compounded by contamination. Those who find themselves thirsty and overwhelmed by the situation will find the consumption of alcohol does not help them rehydrate[183].

Maintaining a case of bottled water per person in your household will enable you to have roughly a gallon of water per person, which may be sufficient for a three-day supply, assuming (24 16 oz bottles per case). Water in disaster areas goes fast because of many non-obvious demands, like hygiene, rehydrating dehydrated foods, and pet hydration. When sufficient bottled water supply is available in a disaster area, you might see a case of water per family member distributed at FEMA PODs (point of distribution); however, it may take a week or so for it to arrive.

A simple yet proven portable personal water filtration device is a GravityWorks Water Filter System[184]. Another way of storing an emergency water supply is to use bulk methods, for example, food-grade Saratoga Farms 5-gallon (~40 lbs each) stackable water storage or 50-gal "barrel"[185] and a Seychelle filter pump[186] along with using H2O ResQ Water Storage Additive[187]. Or build your own water gravity filter, such as a DIY 5-gallon filter[188]. Having bags of playground sand, diatomaceous earth, gravel, and several 5-gallon plastic pails "just in case" is a good start.

Even without a disaster, on average, over 16% of water distributed in municipal water systems is lost[189] due to leaks and other pressure surges (negative pressure transients), which also threaten potability. A minimum of 20 PSI hydrant pressure must be maintained to inhibit infiltration and water potability[190]. A pressure drop can occur for many reasons[191], including broken mains, loss of power, loss of sources of supply, booster pump failure, sudden demands, or other system component failures.

Considering the Earth's atmosphere holds an estimated 12 quintillion liters[192] of water, a more dependable water accumulation practice may be to use a solar-powered atmospheric water generator to provide a completely portable, off-electric-grid, and off-water-grid source of drinking water. For example, as long as your ambient environment is between 41F-90F and the relative humidity is between 35%-90%, a Watergen[193] atmospheric water generator machine could provide up to 10 Liters of potable water a day using 200 Watts*24hrs (4,800Wh) of power. The prototype Technion system[194] and others[195] show promise for even more energy efficiency. For a pragmatic example of water conservation, since 1948, Israel has been able to transform their land, which started to be over 70% desert.[196] Using atmospheric water generation, drip irrigation, desalination (80% of Israel's potable water is derived from energy-intensive desalination[197]), and recycling 90% of its wastewater. In extreme situations, use an absorbent towel to wipe condensed water from clean surfaces, such as with a Shamwow[198].

A small community's water supply needs can be met with a 120 gallons per hour solar-powered filtration system[199] that can take virtually any fresh water source (like a lake or swimming pool) and provide up to 2 gallons a minute of USEPA and NSF P231/P248 compliant potable water. Those with access to healthy well water and not dependent upon a municipal water supply may want to implement a solar microgrid for their home/farm water well, such as an RPS backup and redundant water systems[200].

SEWER
Suppose you are dependent upon using a municipal sewer system that depends on sewer lift stations[201] instead of gravity flowing sanitary sewer lines. In that case, you can be at risk of sewer backup if the pump station's power fails and backup of your neighbor's sewerage into the lower points of your building through the floor drains and basement toilets. One form of contingency planning is to keep a box of 13-gallon plastic bags strategically pre-positioned. Hence, the bags are readily available as impromptu liners for toilets that can no longer flush.

Eventually, the need for outhouses[202] or 5-gallon bucket toilets may emerge as your last resort, necessitating careful planning to prevent ground/stream water contamination and to maintain some level of convenience while remaining downwind from prevailing wind direction over your residence. Educating yourself on the various methods of attempting odor control and aiding decomposition through using lime[203] or yeast and preparing your supplies beforehand is a must.

FOOD

Nonperishable emergency food is essential. Each household should have at least three days (better yet, three months or more) of nonperishable food per person, for example, from sources like LDS Online[204], Heavens Harvest[205], or PatriotSupply[206]. An excellent book, *The Lost SuperFoods*[207], gives great advice on food preservation. One way to store bulk grains and rice is by packing it in food-grade 5-gallon buckets sealed separately in sealable 5-gallon bucket-sized bags with desiccant oxygen absorbers, such as oxygenabsorbers.com[208]. A belt-and-suspenders approach to enhance food preservation can include using nitrogen packing, for example, with Gerneron[209].

Food safety

A final note on food safety is the need to pay attention to safe food handling and preparation guidelines, such as the FDA Safe Food Handling guidelines[210]. About 1 in 6 (48 million) Americans suffer from food poisoning each year, resulting in 128,000 hospitalizations and 3,000 deaths, and this is without a disaster. As an emergency manager, look for volunteers with formal food handling training or certified food protection managers (CFPM) when relying on NGOs or other volunteer organizations for food preparation and distribution in a disaster area.

SHELTER IS THE FOURTH RESPONSE PRIORITY

A few things to consider for home location:

- Greater than 5 miles (or better yet, at least a day's walk) from the nearest Interstate/major roadway and railroad
- The driveway connects to a maintained thoroughfare (perhaps a school bus route?)
- Shared electrical grid with the local fire department (or other public facility)
- Defensible cul-de-sac is ideal
- Good neighbors
- Southern slope

Here are a few things to consider for home selection or preparation:

- 200 Amp service main with craftsman-like wiring
- Ability to island[211] with a solar power supplied system
- All exterior door locks should include deadbolts and be pick-proof, such as using Medeco[212].
- Anti-shatter film[213] on all windows
- Code-compliant home, including use of grounded and CGFI outlets
- Consider a blue metal roof:') (Pantone N20-30/SW 6957? ;')
- Electrical transfer switch[214] and shore power connectors
- Ember-resistant[215] gable/eave vent protection
- Gravity sewer or septic system
- Large underground propane tank (if possible) as natural gas supply will likely become interrupted
- Maintain a minimum 100' defensible space[216] around a home
- Multi-fuel (or at least LP) whole home generator, such as a Generac[217]
- Reinforced garage door
- Water well, gravity water supply (with a storage tank with >80' in elevation preferred)

BUGGING OUT

Your bug out plans should include more than your ill-considered desire to spontaneously share a Superdome refuge experience[218] with 15,000 other people you don't know. Planning well in advance to relocate can enable you to be mentally prepared and relocate with minimum consternation. Joel Skousen's book *Strategic Relocation*[219] is an excellent resource for those looking to relocate.

Conversely, suppose you have a strong aversion to ever bugging out, so you think you won't ever need a bug out bag. However, consider your preparedness if you face a sudden mandatory evacuation,[220] which could become necessary as a protective action to help save lives in emergencies, floods, toxic gas releases, wildfires, mudflows, or other unforeseen events. For example, as of 2018, the CDC reported that eight[221] Southern U.S. states have hurricane evacuation laws, and the level of enforcement of mandatory evacuation[222] varies by state.

While you may feel personally entitled to ignore evacuation advice or orders, potentially to protect your home and possessions, what if the situation worsens? Are you selfishly expecting someone else to endanger themselves to rescue you in unanticipated worsening conditions? Suppose part of your reluctance to leave includes having pets. In that case, it is better to plan and include them in your evacuation plans with a bug out bag of animal food, a water bowl, treats, and a collar/leash.

When you are bugging out, you will have no idea what situations you may face; some may include a combination of being crammed into a crowded bus, on a motorcycle, on the back end of a truck, a small plane, a helicopter, and even a 50-mile hike. Various bag load-outs can be designed for unique scenarios and pre-staged to be readily available when needed. Most critical is when your plans include needing to care for another, including addressing special needs, etc. We have come a long way since the Civil War soldiers' everyday carry (EDC[223]) typically consisted of a comb, sewing kit, and bandana. But nowadays, every ounce quickly adds up, so it is important to focus on minimizing the bag's safe lift[224] weight to keep it under 51 pounds; otherwise, things rapidly get out of hand. Think about it: back in the day, a bandana was in the plan. What has changed to where it seems we are packing so heavy to now need a U-Haul? ;')

When possible, pack in layers, including the everyday carry (EDC) as part of your preparation. Modern EDC may include a flashlight, multi-tool, notepad, and tactical pen with works anywhere ink (www.spacepen.com[225]). Your carry could be as simple as a Fenix Penlight[226] (80 Lumen) and Swisstech Utili-key 6-in-1[227] multitool or as functional as a USB-C rechargeable Fenix PD-36R[228] 1700 Lumen flashlight and a Leatherman Multi-Tool[229]. The reasoning behind having two flashlights for mission-critical lighting is that emergency managers are also wise to have a backup plan when their primary plan goes south; hence, the expression has evolved as two is one, and one is none[230].

What to have in your bug out bag is very situation-dependent, debatable, and extensive. Consider reading the *ReadyMan*[231] *Poor Man's Bug Out Escape & Evasion*[232] (Ross 2023) guide as an excellent place to start. Regarding the variety of bug out bags, these "fantasy lists" can be extensive, including:
- 72-hour kit[233] bag
- CERT kit[234] (Community Emergency Response Team)
- Digital go-bag (Remember, data is comparatively not heavy. Use an encrypted USB drive with PDFs of property tax, insurance, legal documents, contact list, etc.) *Honorable mention for my better half advocating digital go-bags as part of her work over 20 years ago.*
- Emergency kit/bag[235]
- Evacuation bag[236]
- GOOD bag[237] ("Get Out of Dodge")
- INCH bag[238] ("I'm Never Coming Home")

- Shelter Bag[239]
- SHTF bag[240] (defecation hits the rotary oscillator bag)
- Survival bag/kit[241]
- Trauma kit/first aid[242]

LAYERS (ATTIRE, TEMPERATURE, MOBILE)

Extend your thinking beyond your house as your first layer of natural shelter, which starts with the shoes you are wearing and the shirt on your back. Even more importantly, your clothing can prevent you from becoming chilled. Hypothermia can become a killer, even in ~50-65F ambient weather. Staying as dry as possible and wearing serviceable shoes and clothing while dressing in layers is essential to preparation. Your most basic shelter begins by using non-flammable[243] clothing in layers, which may help with your body's thermal regulation and avoid trapping perspiration. Work to blend in by wearing nothing distinctive and maintaining no memorable odor. It is an extension of your personal "everyday carry" to include sturdy shoes, as many boards seem to land with nails pointing up in a disaster area.

Watch where you walk, particularly in heavily flooded areas. People have been known to drop into open, flooded utility holes. Remember, virtually all storm sewer drains flow into rivers, lakes, and retention ponds, and when they, in turn, become flooded, the resulting blowback can be significant. It is not unusual for the resulting hydraulic pressures to lift off utility hole covers.

Consider your vehicle as your mobile cave. To that end, consider buying more resilient cars or trucks, particularly with features such as full-sized spare tires and towing capability. An extra inch or two of road clearance can save your life if you have to drive over fallen branches. Make preventative maintenance a way of life, including treating a half-tank of fuel as empty and half-tread on your tires as effectively bald. A good goal is to keep your vehicle ready to reliably carry all household members, pets, and supplies for at least 50 miles at any moment's notice (effectively at least two days' walk away[244]). Extend the everyday carry model to your vehicle, as it can become your lifeboat in a disaster. Think what having three days of U.S. Coast Guard (USCG[245]) approved food and water (for example, five-year shelf life Datrex[246] emergency food rations and water pouches), as well as a bunch of thermal mylar space blankets[247], a fire extinguisher, trauma/first-aid[248] kit, automotive hand tools such as an Irwin Vise-Grip Multi-Tool[249], another flashlight, saltwater capable water filter like a Katadyn Survivor 35[250], and a mobile 12V 400-watt power inverter.

SURVIVAL SHELTER

If your home is uninhabitable but you are not faced with having to bug out, and if your home continues to have a working sewer, or even better, potable water and electrical supply, then explore your options of securing a travel trailer or mobile home to park adjacent to your home to provide better security for your home and reduce the probability of thieves stealing the copper wire and piping[251]. It may be prudent to have some essential materials on hand in case of damage to your roof, windows, etc. Temporary repair materials can include 20'x100' rolls of Black and Clear 6 mil or heavier poly plastic sheeting, tarps, duct tape[252], and rope[253]. For example, a game changer is the ability to cover the roof quickly after losing all your shingles and blocking any subsequent rain from soaking down through your home.

Depending on your circumstances and budget, you may have to use a temporary survival shelter, typically as simple as a lean-to, teepee, A-Frame, or hammock. At the same time, you may also need to try to remain inconspicuous, particularly by paying attention to any lighting you may need to use at night. The ingenuity and experience of numerous homeless people may be well worth learning from.

FIVE DISASTER MANAGEMENT STAGES

Manage resources better by breaking the lifecycle of a disaster into five stages[254]: **prevention, mitigation, preparedness, response, and recovery**.

Prevention

Prevention is working to avoid or minimize creating a hazard or event from being a risk in the first place. Political corruption involving prevention can exacerbate a disaster. For example, Dr. Jordan Peterson writes about Katrina: *"The Dutch prepare their dikes for the worst storm in ten thousand years. Had New Orleans followed that example, no tragedy would have occurred. It's not that no one knew. The Flood Control Act of 1965 mandated improvements in the levee that held back Lake Pontchartrain. The system was to be completed by 1978. Forty years later, only 60 percent of the work had been done. Willful blindness and corruption took the City down."* (Peterson 2018)

Mitigation (both before and after the disaster or event)

Mitigation helps remove or lessen a potential disaster's negative natural and social impact. Political and financial intrigue often compounds the confusion between prevention and pre-disaster mitigation because of instances where there may be economic advantages in delaying investment in prevention. At the same time, certain parties take advantage of the situation to exploit the lack of prevention. For example, mitigation could be as simple as dredging, improving drainage ditches, or installing shatterproof glass. However, the concepts of "navigable waters" and "watershed" frequently are political footballs because of the amount of money involved for dredging (and the lack thereof) and the grab for land rights being expanded to include drainage ditches, culverts, and control of the farmer's field drainage tiling. For example, the impact of the political battle to withdraw the spending for dredging to maintain the navigable waters of a portion of West Virginian rivers became apparent with their subsequent severe flooding. One West Virginian bemoaned no longer hearing the riverboat calliope. Others reflected on the flooding and the loss of the damaged road and railroad bridges.

Preparedness

Manage risk by performing a continuous cycle of planning, organizing, training, equipping, exercising, evaluating, and mitigating to respond to all potential disasters.

Response

While meeting basic human needs after an incident, responding quickly to save lives and protect property and the environment can be critically important. The ability to respond with a coordinated search and rescue is constrained by the survivor's condition, stamina, level of dehydration, and resource constraints. Typically, survivors cannot go without water for more than three days and rarely more than a week, after which a disaster response typically turns into a recovery.

Recovery

Typically, recovery begins immediately after the threat to human life has subsided. Through a focus on the timely restoration, strengthening, and revitalization of infrastructure, housing, and a sustainable economy, the health, social, cultural, historical, and environmental fabric of affected communities can move towards some semblance of a "new normal."

SIX DISASTER EMOTIONAL REACTION PHASES

The six disaster emotional reaction phases are often confused with psychiatrist Elisabeth Kubler-Ross's stages of grief[255] (denial, anger, bargaining, depression, and acceptance). The latter more accurately reflects a series of common experiences rather than required experiences. To better understand and help those affected by a disaster, it may be helpful to be aware of the emotional reaction of the survivors and how that may help optimize your interaction with them. Disaster emotional responses may reflect the phase of the disaster they are experiencing and can typically be viewed as one of six phases of emotional reaction[256]: **PRE-DISASTER, IMPACT, HEROIC, HONEYMOON, DISILLUSIONMENT, and RECOVERY.**

PRE-DISASTER PHASE
For those affected, the pre-disaster phase may be severe enough to simply form the baseline from which the rest of their life will never be the same. If the incident comes without warning, they may feel a debilitating lack of security. In contrast, if the incident occurs with the luxury of notice, then a pending sense of loss of control or doom may cloud their judgment, leave them feeling guilty or second-guessing, and fill them with self-blame for previous poor decision-making and execution.

IMPACT PHASE
Usually, the quickest moving phase, where shock, panic, disbelief, and confusion can create intense emotional reactions focused on self-preservation and family, particularly for those without relevant experience or training. Because of falling trees, power lines, and flying debris, it is unsafe to be outside when sustained winds exceed 39 mph, particularly if gusts exceed 57 mph. It was a sobering lesson when a sheet of siding flew by, halving a wooden pole beside me. Also, attempting to walk or drive in moving flood waters is unsafe. You can't help anyone later if you become a victim in the aptly titled impact phase, so set the right example for safety first.

HEROIC PHASE
After the initial impact of the disaster has become internalized, many may be moved by a sense of altruism where their risk assessment ability may be reduced, and they exhibit selfless adrenaline-induced rescue behavior. Some may say this is where they have "brass balls," and others become "Mama Bears," which actually may be attributable to their larger-than-average amygdalae glands[257] at the base of their skull. They may also be significantly more responsive to seeing somebody else in distress. Some of the greatest heroes are the unassuming emergency managers, who, through their selfless giving of their time, energy, and abilities, stay on task as the disaster unfolds around them.

HONEYMOON PHASE
During the first few weeks of a response to a disaster, there is often an unrealistic rush to recover, and it is easy to over-promise and under-deliver. For example, when the electricity service has been partially restored, but the storm debris is still clogging the curb, the trash removal service has yet to be restarted. The disaster honeymoon phase is frequently a euphoric time where community cohesion lends itself towards a great sense of optimism, even while the individuals impacted have yet to experience recovery. The individual's failure to share in the recovery can devastate and drag the entire community down. Emergency managers should keep aware of those left behind and falling into depression. It is not a time to adopt a cheerleader attitude to fix the problem; rather, it is time to help survivors get plugged into resources larger than themselves.

DISILLUSIONMENT PHASE

After the honeymoon phase of unrealistic expectations wears off, many communities and individuals realize the limits of potential disaster assistance. The increasing gap between actual needs and potentially falling aid levels may lead to adverse reactions and feelings of abandonment. Many may have trigger events that remind them of the disastrous events that lead them toward their new normal. It is critical to focus on doing something positive towards their new normal rather than focus on depression or unconstructive acts. In particular, this can be a treacherous time for recovering people with substance use disorder and unstable marriages.

RECOVERY PHASE

As the community and individuals start to come to terms with their new normal, a premature sense of recovery may emerge. This is when forward thinking and planning are needed to inspire positive changes to disrupt any harmful return to a potentially undesirable status quo. The recovery phase is best when insurance and recovery money are spent on modernizing infrastructure and meeting updated construction codes rather than replacing unnecessary items. For example, when a homeowner unnecessarily pays a portion of their homeowner insurance check to replace their now grown daughter's childhood bicycle lost in the disaster because they were used to seeing it in the garage.

LOGISTICS

Shortages are inherent in a disaster, so prepping in times of abundance is the right thing to do. Even the Pharaoh prepared for bad times by storing grain in good times. Saving in preparation is not a sin, but hoarding during a disaster is. The power law of distribution empirically applies in many situations where roughly 80% of effects come from 20% of incidents, and approximately 80% of the injuries are caused by 20% of the hazards (Pareto principle[258].) The law of diminishing returns starts to become apparent when you over-prepare by trying to prepare for everything, and you discover your costs and maintenance of the preparation effort rapidly become prohibitive. Realistically, you may find that 20% of your prepping effort applies to at least 80% of the hazards you may face.

While the military focuses on delivering the right munition and other supplies to the right place at the right time, they fully understand that logistics dictates what is possible and what is not[259]. Meanwhile, FEMA helps coordinate 15 emergency support functions (ESFs)[260] to "deliver the right resources, at the right place, at the right time, to support state, local, tribal and territorial governments[261]." It is an arduous task in its own right to manage logistics storage and staging in a disaster area. FEMA is assigned to Emergency Support Function (ESF) #7[262], providing logistics integration for whole community logistics incident planning and support for timely and efficient delivery of supplies, equipment, services, and facilities. It also facilitates comprehensive logistics planning, technical assistance, training, education, exercise, incident response, and sustainment that leverage the capability and resources of federal logistics partners, public and private stakeholders, and nongovernmental organizations (NGOs) in support of both responders and disaster survivors.

A simple list from FEMA to get you started on basic logistic supplies is available from ready.gov: FEMA Ready.Gov Emergency Supply List[263] as part of the overall FEMA Ready Gov Kit[264].

Basic Ready.Gov emergency supply list
- Water and non-perishable food for several days
- Extra cell phone battery or charger
- Battery-powered or hand crank radio that can receive NOAA Weather Radio tone alerts and extra batteries
- Flashlight and extra batteries
- First-aid kit
- Whistle (to signal for help)
- Dust mask (to help filter contaminated air)
- Plastic sheeting and duct tape to shelter in place
- Moist towelettes, garbage bags, and plastic ties for personal sanitation
- Non-sparking (such as brass) wrench or pliers to turn off utilities
- Can opener
- Local maps

Additional items to consider
- Prescription medications and glasses
- Infant formula and diapers
- Pet food, water, and supplies for your (or lost) pet(s)

- Important family documents, such as copies of insurance policies, identification, and bank account records, in a portable waterproof container
- Cash and quarters
- Emergency reference material such as a first-aid book or information
- A warm blanket[265] or sleeping bag for each person. Consider additional bedding if you live in a cold-weather climate
- Complete change of clothing, including a long-sleeved shirt, long pants, and sturdy shoes.
- Consider additional clothing if you live in a cold-weather environment.
- Fire extinguisher
- Matches in a waterproof container
- Feminine supplies, personal hygiene items, and hand sanitizer
- Mess kits, paper cups, plates and disposable utensils, paper towels
- Paper and pencil
- Books, games, puzzles, or other activities for children

Sometimes, seemingly complex logistic challenges can be simplified by asking the right question. For example, after Hurricane Sandy, gas stations were closed in over twenty New Jersey counties, and the management team requested building a list of those that were closed (assuming they were out of gas). But it proved much more helpful to know why they were closed! Were they closed because of a lack of fuel, electricity, labor, or damage?

Where possible, work towards a broader solution instead of focusing on what appears to be a simple, one-time, temporary solution. For example, an emergency request was received for a 5-gallon can of gas for a small special-needs hospital in NJ during Hurricane Sandy. It became apparent the actual issue was completely different when it turned into attempting to keep track of the consumption and keeping them from running out of fuel for their generator. It proved much more straightforward for FEMA to task a fuel truck to deliver 1,000 gallons for the local small town's storage tank used for their snow truck fuel. This fuel could then be used to service frequent local re-supply to the hospital's 5-gallon fuel cans and simultaneously address the other local under-serviced municipal disaster-related fuel needs in the area.

The most essential truth in disaster logistics for an emergency manager is the importance of expectation management. Simply put, never imply any commitment you are not confident you can deliver. It is significantly better to under-promise and be able to over-deliver. As a word of caution, never promise to provide what you cannot or do not intend to keep.

For example, consider the importance of managing the parking lot for an incident response gathering. Proper spacing, access, and egress of the vehicles and any safety-related considerations, including the occupant's special needs and access requirements, animals, and potentially hazardous cargo, are essential to anticipate. In particular, in case of a large disaster, include a capability to handle semi-trailer parking. As a rule of thumb, plan for 120-foot long by 20-foot wide drive-through spaces so a truck never has to back up. An ideal large disaster logistics marshalling yard could be an unused airport taxiway's large concrete paved area. Remember that the loaded weight of a semi-truck of bottled water could easily be 65,000–80,000 pounds, which could destroy an asphalt surface when parked for any duration.

The author found it highly beneficial to add the following impromptu disaster response kit to his rental vehicle before responding to a disaster response area:

- 300-page account book[266], enabling indelible legal record-keeping
- Area and state folding maps (from AAA[267], truck stops[268], etc.)
- Case (or two) of bottled water[269]
- Case of Charmin toilet paper[270] (individual or sub-packaging preferred)
- Case of Snickers bars[271] (great high-energy emergency nourishment and balancing living off MREs)
- Cases of fig Newtons[272] (great for encounters with children with concerned parents in a disaster area)
- Several Scotch 810[273] Magic Tape, 3/4 x 1296", 1" Core (to tape in business cards, etc.)
- Several Uniball Signo 207[274] 33951 Gel Pen, 0.7mm Medium Point, Blue Uni Super Ink (indelible, unique color ink, stands out during any photocopying or legal review)
- ABC fire extinguisher[275]
- First-aid kit[276]

Finally, the most important thing to consider in your ultimate logistic planning is the final destination of your Soul.

LOGISTICS – MULTIPLIERS

When logistic materials are at a premium, the two critical significant logistics multipliers are:
1. Preparation (anticipation before the fact logistics), and
2. Communications

Preparation

Suppose resource limitations narrow your scope of preparation. In that case, you can still simply rely on JOY, which, when selflessly applied, can act as a considerable resource multiplier when resources are hard to come by. Unbelievers, including many billionaires, are building underground bunkers[277] in their ignorance of prophecy, and these bunkers can cost between $60,00 to more than $9M[278]. However, when your neighbor knocks, are you prepared to help even if they may not reciprocate?

Communications

The ability to exchange (or at least receive) data (which has unique intangible qualities like having no mass) is a significant logistics multiplier. Radios, field phones, and full telecommunications, including satellite, cell, landline, and facsimile (FAX), can enhance your disaster response. Even without reliable Internet and cellular communications, two-way radio can simplify the logistics of information, share digital data, and streamline logistics distribution.

Many people are building their communications systems dependent on the Internet (and the phone system, which is becoming increasingly reliant on the Internet). However, many remain oblivious that sovereign Internet control has already been given to the U.N.[279] In the time leading up to the Tribulation, people will learn that the Internet will increasingly be centrally controlled and a tool for the Antichrist's emerging one-world form of government and monetary system. Eventually, some global equity tax will appear, based on your IP address (or other unique identifier). As such, it will become part of the prophetically foretold system that no one can live without its capabilities, which will complicate your ability to use it when responding to an emergency.

As your budget permits, having a battery-operated compact AM/FM/NOAA/shortwave radio can provide access to receiving valuable information, including weather reports, and considerably improve your situational awareness. In particular, a National Oceanic and Atmospheric (NOAA) capable radio can provide hydrologic and climate forecasts and local inclement weather warnings[280]. AM radios will enable you to monitor AM broadcast stations that are part of the National Emergency Alert System.

A shortwave radio is helpful for time signals, national/international news, and situation reports from shortwave broadcast stations in many languages. For example, consider tuning to WRMI in Florida at 9.955 MHz or WBCQ at 7.490, 9.330, 5.130, 7.265, or 6.160 MHz. Choice of radios can include (~$70) Midland ER310 Weather Radio[281], (~$200) C.CRANE CC Skywave SSB2[282], (~$200) Eton Elite Executive Radio[283], or (~$800) Icom IC-R30[284]. Other shortwave radio brands include Ten-Tec 1254 kit/RX-340 or a high-end Rhode & Schwartz brand radio. A great HF frequency chart to print out and keep for when the power is out is from C.CRANE[285]. However, remember that any radio with microelectronics produced in China may have a higher microelectronics pulse vulnerability[286] (He 2019), including fused circuits baked into their exported microelectronics.

The challenges you face in maintaining reliable two-way communications are not comparable to the capabilities of one-way commercial AM and FM broadcast stations, as their transmitters may use thousands or millions of Watts and 1,000-foot high antennas. As avid audiophiles have learned, half of the cost for a great stereo is typically in the speakers. The same kind of lesson applies to reliable two-way radio communications, where the cost and sophistication of your antenna and associated components may easily match the cost of your radio.

If your situation devolves towards black sky conditions[287], you may have to rely on radio communications to maintain or enhance your logistics capabilities. Radio is useful for both one-way information distribution (which can be as simple as a community using a high-powered AM transmitter and individual unpowered crystal radio receivers[288] with its high impedance earphone) or having a two-way communications capability using various forms, including obtaining an FCC amateur radio license and the necessary antenna/radio equipment, and using Morse code[289] (to overcome high radio background noise environments) or various digital operating modes[290] , which can use computer-based applications to exchange emails and share .csv data files, for example, using Winlink[291]. amateur radio, with its digital modes, is a unique significant asset. Amateur radio can become much more helpful if your family, friends, and essential contacts are similarly prepared, enabling you to communicate without the Internet and phone.

It may take quite a bit of effort and investment to maintain reliable two-way communications:

- **"Neighborhood-wide" communications** cost ~$160 for a pair of FRS/GRMS radios. These simple, short-ranged ultra-high frequency (UHF) FRS/GRMS handheld radios may enable you to communicate around your neighborhood without opening your door. For example, a pair of (~$160) waterproof Motorola T600[292] radios from Walmart uses USB-C rechargeable or disposable AA batteries, which include a flashlight and NOAA receiver capability function. Using FRS band radios does not require an FCC license. While the advertised range in the brochure looks nice, it is prudent to consider it measured more from a proverbial unobstructed mountaintop to the next mountaintop. Verify you can establish an all hands situational net with your neighborhood watch team to understand its limitations better. After Hurricane Sandy, FRS radios were successfully used for supply line communications in portions of NYC.

- **County-wide communications** cost ~$500 using SSB over CB. Citizens band (CB)[293] radios provide a step towards using more extended range high frequency (HF) two-way plain-language voice communications. CB radio enables intercommunication with other similarly equipped stations. The typical mobile-capable CB radio does not require a license. It can operate on 12 V DC from your vehicle's cigarette lighter jack. Channel 9 is commonly monitored for emergency communications and traveler assistance, and Channel 19 is used as an open call channel for trucker/vehicle intercommunications.

  CB radios are regulated to transmit with no more than 4 watts transmitter carrier output power when using amplitude modulation (AM). A rough rule of thumb for the probable range is an average of a watt per mile. This means that, when using ground wave (not ionospheric skip), you may typically expect up to a 3–5 mile range. However, stepping up to a radio that supports single-sideband (SSB) modulation, which can legally transmit with 12 watts peak envelope power (PEP), can typically enable an effective range of 10–15 miles. Selecting upper sideband (USB) on HF on CB is customary. For example, a (~$200) Uniden 980 SSB[294] radio, coupled with a quality external base antenna[295], quality coaxial antenna cable[296], and an EMP-rated lightning arrester[297] (costing around $500), can typically enable local neighborhood to neighborhood level radio communications.

  The author used a handheld CB radio to help expedite the marshaling of an unanticipated semi-truck convoy arriving at a disaster marshaling yard at night. It made completing the task much safer and quicker, and return to sleep;').

- **State-wide communications** costing ~$1,000 using amateur radio (HAM) HF 100-watt HF transceivers or 2/440 V HF/UHF with repeaters is possible. Many think they would like to add an amateur radio capability as their ultimate solution because it can enable global communications (depending on the equipment, antenna, skills, and conditions). However, it also requires a serious commitment, skills, license, and having to live where you can raise an antenna. A big plus for amateur radio is the ability to exchange digital data over the air. If you are interested in getting licensed and learning more about amateur radio (and becoming a "Ham"), a great place to start is at the Amateur Radio Relay League (ARRL[298]) website. Once you have your license, you may want to complete your online emergency communications (EmComm[299]) training, which is available through the ARRL.

  The shorter-ranged VHF, UHF, and SHF bands offer many unique attributes, including community-minded operators and clubs who have repeaters and are often focused on the 2 meter (144 MHz) VHF and   meter (420 MHz) UHF bands. An underutilized privilege available to the entry-level Technician Class licensee[300] is the 10 meter HF band. This can be used for many modes, including data, RTTY, and SSB at up to 200 watts PEP.

- **Multi-state-wide (or more) communications** costing ~$3,000, $10,000 or more, using amateur radio (HAM) HF 100-watt HF transceiver, and optionally with a linear amplifier is also possible. Amateur radio operators can transmit across most HF bands using up to 1,500 watts of PEP[301]. While it is possible to opportunistically communicate worldwide with a simple wire antenna and low power, those who step up their game with towers and high-gain directional antennas can have greater confidence in making reliable connections. It is also important to remember that using higher transmitting power becomes problematic when using battery/emergency power.

The most significant barriers restraining amateur radio use are the predominant forms of common-interest development[302] rental agreements and ordinances restricting or impacting the installation of outdoor antennas. About half of all U.S. homes and virtually all apartments are now governed by antenna prohibitions (except for satellite dishes for some reason). This has had a chilling effect on the use of HF radio in particular and inhibits the growth of communication expertise and emergency communications capability. An example of how contentious antenna restrictions can become is when a neighbor within a California homeowners association (HOA[303]) became so zealous that they took it upon themselves to enforce antenna restrictions by cutting a temporary antenna coax being used to provide emergency communications in support of an isolated fire truck in a deep ravine fighting a California wildfire. Fortunately, no lives were lost, but the TV News truck accompanying the fire truck was destroyed.

Some preppers have expressed concern[304] because all FCC amateur radio[305] licensees are listed[306] publicly[307] on the Internet. There is a history of governments confiscating[308] radio transmitters (and, at times, even receivers[309]), so there is a reluctance to receive the necessary training and an amateur radio license. (It could be viewed as a safety-threatening situation similar to the challenges of gun registration.) However, modern radio direction finding[310], software-defined radio (SDR[311]), and drone RDF technology[312] advances make efforts to conduct previously hard-to-detect and locate radio communication very difficult.

DISASTER RISK CONSIDERATIONS

NATURAL DISASTERS

Between 1980–2024, the U.S. experienced over 395 weather/climate[313] natural disasters exceeding $1B in damages. Tropical cyclones (hurricanes) losses totaled $850B, drought losses totaled $236B, and severe storm losses totaled another $206B. Preparing for the most common natural disaster in your state is prudent. So, while tornadoes have happened in all of the continental United States over the past 100 years, they are most common in only 12 states. Meanwhile, tropical cyclones (hurricanes) are more common in 13 other states, and wildfires are more common in yet another 11.[314]

GRID DOWN (CME, CYBER, DEW, EMP, KINETIC)

There is an increasing danger of a regional or the national electric grid being shut down as a result of a major coronal mass ejection (CME)[315], cyberattack, directed-energy weapon, electromagnetic pulse (EMP)[316], or kinetic attack (such as destroying multiple interdependent power station transformers). Any of these can then put America back into the horse and buggy era without the horse and buggy. These potentially black sky[317] events will likely also become sovereignty-threatening events. China, Russia, and other aggressive actors will likely offer assistance without any intention to leave, which then confronts the U.S. government having to choose between either starvation or capitulation of its citizens.

Where we once had nearly half of the population working full-time in agriculture back in the 1880s, we now have no more than half of America with gardens and only 2% working full-time in agriculture. The country will suddenly have an urgent need for innovation to be able to feed itself, likely through aggressive adoption of hydroponics (likely Kratky), vertical gardening (possibly leveraging beneficial nematodes and other radical soil nutrition breakthroughs), using non-GMO heirloom seeds, and very efficient animal husbandry.

In a long-term grid down situation, our national lifestyle will return to the 1880s rural horse and buggy pre-electrification era without having many horses and buggies. Potable water, food, medicine, brass, and lead will become extremely valuable. While before the Rapture, the price of gold may rise past $5,000, remember it will be considered worthless and unclean during the Great Tribulation (Ezekiel 7:19). This will likely become true because of the use of super-spreader diseases like SARS, Ebola, Marburg, or their derivatives. Because of the growing menace of bacteriological, viral, chemical, and radiological threats, there is coming a time when the exchange of cash and coins will not even be possible and will be considered illegal. The WEF will likely eliminate the use of money and gold by labeling them as fomite surfaces[318] that contribute to the transmission of diseases.

As dependence on the declining production of food (and farming) becomes critical, about 2 million American active/reserve/guard Armed Force members plus 1.5 million emergency responders (totaling roughly 1% of the U.S. population) will need varying levels of food and support to enable them to focus on their work, and at the same time the rest of America will return to food production in a primitive agrarian economy, without refrigeration and modern tools.

CME

A coronal mass ejection[319] is a large expulsion of magnetized plasma from the Sun, which can have a severe geomagnetic impact on satellites, radio communication, the Internet, and the national electric grid.[320] The most significant CME in recorded history was the 1859 Carrington Event[321], which seriously impacted the telegraph system. A similar event today would likely destroy the national electric grid[322] and should be considered similar to an EMP E3 component. While a large CME is an infrequent event, it presents a potentially highly catastrophic consequence given today's dependency on electricity.

CYBER

The U.S. electric grid is susceptible to cyberattacks[323]. It is a highly interdependent system[324] comprising over 3,300 utilities, 200,000 miles of high-tension lines, 55,000 substations, and 5.5 million miles of distribution lines. Most systems are remotely monitored and controlled using industrial control systems with bolt-on modernized cybersecurity capability. Compounding the situation is the absence of manual controls and a few skilled operators, making moving to manual control of the grid[325] a difficult last resort option.

While the DoD and a few other organizations have been adopting microgrids[326] and small modular reactors[327](SMR), and while SMRs may be beyond the average pocketbook at least for the time being;'), everyone should adopt a microgrid approach as soon as possible. Budget permitting, one way to start could be as simple as installing a solar household power system, such as a Tesla Powerwall[328] or Generac PWRcell[329]. DYI examples include Big Battery Ethos System[330], Victron Energy[331], and Dakota Lithium[332].

Start moving towards a grid-independent lifestyle, even if you can only start using rechargeable batteries, a small solar charger, and an outdoor cooking grill. Effective personal cybersecurity starts with keeping all your installed software current, regularly completing archives written to removable write-once-read-many (WORM[333]) media such as CD or Blu-Ray disks, and maintaining backups of your data on hard drives you control. Accessing data in the cloud will become impossible in a grid-down event, particularly if the LEO satellite network systems are disrupted.

DEW

Directed-energy weapons[334] can be deployed in many forms, including directed acoustic energy, which was historically used as a form of crowd control by making people uncomfortable. Early DEW used to be typically intended for nonlethal intermediate force capability (IFC). Directed microwave energy weapons (akin to Havana syndrome[335]) appear to be featured in the civil war highlighted in former President Obama's *Leave The World Behind*[336]. Offhand, we may find a tinfoil hat solution that might work to help protect from pulsed microwave energy weapons like those used in a Havana syndrome-type attack.

Other forms of DEW include lasers, which have been used by the CCP against pilots[337], and directed-high-energy-pulse weapons, including a non-nuclear electromagnetic pulse weapon[338] (NNEMP) and flux compression generator bomb[339] (FCGs). These can create a high-power microwave pulse to destroy anything with electronics in the target area. Several of the directed-energy weapon system designs have been publicly known for over 50 years, so while refined and powerful weapon implementations are in production with nation-states, it is not too far of a stretch for members of the general population to fall victim to use of the weapon type by terrorists and malcontents.

EMP

Any 3 kT to 3 MT nuclear explosion detonated above 25 miles (~40 km) altitude generates several types of EMP components that will impact electrical and connected electronic systems over large regions. An EMP attack has three components[340]:

- E1 is produced when gamma radiation from the nuclear detonation knocks ~10^{25} electrons out of their orbits in atoms in the upper atmosphere and, in turn, impacts the affected area with a brief 200 nanosecond 50 kV x 48 A per square meter pulse.
- E2 is an intermediate time (1 micro to 1 second, 40–120 kV x 5–200 kA) pulse like a lightning strike.
- E3 results from the Earth's electromagnetic field being heaved out of the way and its return. This process, which can take up to hundreds of seconds, results in complex, slow waves of (38–102 V/km[341]) quasi-DC energy currents induced along many conductors across the Earth, including any at the bottom of the ocean and the Earth's core itself. Severe CME has similar effects to E3.

According to the *Electromagnetic Pulse Protection and Resilience Guidelines for Critical Infrastructure and Equipment*[342], civilians can adopt level one of the guidelines as minimum protection

1. Unplug power, data, and antenna lines from spare equipment where feasible.
2. Turn off equipment that cannot be unplugged and is not actively being used.
3. Use at least a lightning-rated surge protection device (SPD) on power cords, antenna lines, and data cables. Maintain a couple of spare SPDs, just in case.
4. Have either EMP-protected backup power or a generation source not connected to the grid with at least one week of on-site fuel or equivalent (e.g., renewable source).
5. Wrap spare electronics with aluminum foil or put them in Faraday containers.

When following the *Department of Energy (DOE) EMP Resilience Plan*[343], and even after adopting a level one "hardening" and Faraday bag[344] approach, actual resilience becomes problematical for civilians because of the uncertainty when facing a no-notice preemptive attack, which will likely involve three (or more) EMP strikes in succession, spread over hours or even weeks. The best way to increase the reliability of your electrical devices and vehicle is by protecting against EMP, lightning, power surges, and solar flare/CME by adding EMP shield[345] protection. In addition, a DEFCON[346] device, a simple plug-in wall-wart type device, provides an audible alarm if an electromagnetic pulse (EMP) or a solar coronal mass ejection (CME) event is detected.

KINETIC

The national electric grid is susceptible to attacks on transformer yards and electric transmission and distribution systems. For example, a sniper[347] disrupted power for a portion of Metcalf, California[348]. The Federal Energy Regulatory Commission (FERC) study indicated that an attack on less than ten power substations[349] could result in taking down the national electric grid. Compounding the growing threat level is the expanding sophistication of possible drone and Molotov cocktail attacks. (Observe the use of asymmetrical weapons (such as drones) in Ukraine.)

Regardless of the cause of the downing of the grid, prudent preparation includes at least having simple multi-use things like maintaining a stock of food, water, and other supplies, and a battery-operated AM/FM/NOAA radio to receive emergency alerts. Depending on your various affiliations, you may want to enroll for the Wireless Priority Service (WPS[350]) phone services and subscribe to the Government

Emergency Telecommunication Services (GETS[351]), if available. Meanwhile, emergency responders should consider land mobile radios[352] with standalone capability, HF radios, and FirstNet[353] (although FirstNet depends upon the continued availability of commercial cellular LTE-Band 14 spectrum service.)

CBRN (CHEMICAL, BIOLOGICAL, RADIOLOGICAL, NUCLEAR)

Historically, CBRN threats used to be considered potential threats between belligerent nations. But now they are increasingly being used asymmetrically by terrorist organizations such as the Tokyo subway sarin[354] gas attack and the attack in Damascus, assumed to be led by the Syrian Government[355].

CBRN threats used to be formerly considered military-grade threats, but now civilians are being hard-pressed to prepare to protect against these forms of attacks. A few have come up with creative and low-cost solutions besides prompt evacuation. It may be most appropriate for civilians on an austere budget who want to prepare for possible CBRN-related incidents to follow the KISS principle, where basic education centers on recognizing threats using the situation and interpreting what is being sensed to evacuate quickly and safely. Few extraordinarily well-prepared preppers have gone the extra measure and procured gas masks, but few (outside the military or hazardous response teams[356]) have gone through the requisite training. Considering a light air breeze[357] (1–3 miles per hour) can carry dangerous material over the distance of a football field in under a minute[358], one of the most critical CBRN preparations is to have a suitable windsock[359] or flag/pennant made of very lightweight material, mounted where it is easy to see, enabling you to quickly determine which direction you can safely travel upwind away from the threat.

CHEMICAL

While the world is officially free of chemical weapons stockpiles[360] according to the OPCW[361], numerous agents continue to be available, ranging from riot control through bear spray. However, accidentally using bleach and ammonia products can create chloramine gas[362] (more commonly referred to as mustard gas[363]) with potentially deadly consequences. Other toxic materials can be accidentally made by mixing bleach and rubbing alcohol, which creates chloroform, and bleach and vinegar can produce chlorine gas.

After a disastrous storm, it is essential to segregate mucked-out[364] kitchen, laundry, and bathroom supplies based on their critical ingredients. In particular, it is a grave mistake not to separate bleach materials. Do not randomly gather and aggregate all bottled materials to place them out to the curb, which can lead to (sometimes literal) cleanup headaches. Amazingly, the National Academy of Engineering (NDRC) *Toxic and Contaminant Concerns Generated by Hurricane Katrina*[365] summary indicates that even after all the destruction in Katrina, the residual localized chemical contamination was minimal years later.

Have you ever wondered what the hazardous materials/dangerous goods identification numbers on the trucks and train cars indicate regarding potential hazards, public safety, emergency response, initial isolation, and protective action distances? An excellent resource is a copy of a current USDOT[366] *Emergency Response Guidebook*[367] (U.S. Government Printing Office 2024) reference book.

BIOLOGICAL

Biological hazards include bacteria, viruses, fungi (including yeasts and molds), and internal human parasites (endoparasites). The importation of exotic rodents as pets leading to monkeypox and SARS by using exotic civet cats for meat are outlined in *The Law of Emergencies*[368] (Hunter 2018). Anthrax has been easy to grow and distribute[369] but has proven difficult to turn into a weapon of mass destruction. The growing experimentation using emerging technologies such as CRISPR[370] is increasing the complexity of detection and remedy. Common modes of transmission include various bodily fluids (including blood, fecal, urine, and saliva) and contact (including sweat, semen, and cervical fluid). Transmission of biological hazards is typically airborne, bodily fluids, and fomite (commonly touched) surfaces. For example, when Ebola was finally declared as effectively a sexually transmitted disease because of its predominant form of transmission, the impact was dramatic on emergency management.

There is a growing awareness that several hundred varieties of fungi (including yeasts and molds) are harmful and deadly[371] to human health. For example, black mold[372] is an example of a natural biological hazard common after flooding. It flourishes in warm water-damaged cellulose materials commonly found in paper/wood products and drywall. FEMA guidance[373] refers to using N95 face masks to help against respiratory distress during cleanup. It also suggests using a full gas mask to include eye protection where needed. According to the National Academy of Engineering (NDRC) *Toxic and Contaminant Concerns Generated by Hurricane Katrina* report, "Unlike air, water, and soil contamination, there is little scientific basis for evaluating the potential effects of mold on human health or for developing risk-based action or cleanup levels. Mold counts of 50,000 spores/m³ are considered very high; spore counts as high as 650,000 spores/m³ were observed by NRDC in a home in mid-city New Orleans (NRDC, 2005a). Because there are no standards to which these mold counts can be compared, there is no clear regulatory responsibility among federal agencies for indoor air. High mold counts are a cause for concern; however, NRDC and EPA recommend that returning residents use respiratory protection and remove all porous construction materials (including carpets and drywall) from flooded homes."

RADIOLOGICAL
Alexander Litvinenko was the first confirmed victim of lethal polonium-210-induced acute radiation syndrome[374] when he effectively starved to death after the lining of his gastrointestinal tract was killed by ingested radiation. Use an effective drinking water filter to reduce radioactive fallout intake from drinking water after a radiological event.

NUCLEAR
One of the lessons reinforced by the Chernobyl disaster is the risk of depending on incident detectors that don't scale adequately. They had radiation detectors in use at the time that indicated low radiation, while the actual radiation levels were beyond the devices' capacity, indicating an incorrect local response. Often compounding the difficulty of remaining safe are other factors involving family and community. For personal radiation detection, the NukAlert[375] is a simple pocket personal radiation meter, monitor, and alarm that gives you a series of chirps when exposed to more than background radiation.

CHAOS and MANUFACTURED DISASTER
From Genesis[376] to Revelation[377], the Bible's central theme is marked by cosmos (through God's holy character) to chaos (introduced by Satan). Even using a scientific approach of chaos theory[378] helps illustrate Satan's deceit through matters seemingly random and unpredictable behavior (effectively Brownian motion). The consequence is highlighted through the frustration of many scientists as they try to prove otherwise, only to rediscover the scientific inerrancy of the Bible written thousands of years ago.

The primary cause of chaos is the evil inspired by Satan (the father of lies[379]). Authoritarian governments and terrorists amplify this evil, and much of the chaos today is through them. The word choice chart below helps to illustrate the dichotomy.

Catastrophe (God's doing)	**Chaos** (Demonic intent)
Liberty	Equality
Wisdom	Stupidity
Mercy	Merciless
Truth	Deceit, censorship
Selflessness, giving, benevolence	Selfishness, greed, love of money
Freedom, accountability	Power, coercion, bribery, blackmail, unaccountability
Right to life, self-defense, family	"Choice", weapon control, socialism
Love, compassion, kindness	Lust, without humanity (Neom), cruelty

ADDITIONAL RESOURCES

Resources for enhancing emergency manager skills

- FEMA *Are You Ready?, An in-depth Guide to Citizen Preparedness,* focusing on CERT, Citizens Corps, over 30 other resources and organizations, and 30 independent study courses through the Emergency Management Institute. (Federal Emergency Management Agency 2020)

- The *Mitigation Strategies for FEMA Command, Control, and Communications During and after a Solar Superstorm* (Winks 2020) unpublished FEMA Report

- *Left of Bang* (Riley 2014), *How the Marine Corps Combat Hunter Program Can Save Your Life* has valuable insight to help managers broaden their situational awareness skills.

- *Leading at a Higher Level* (Blanchard 2010) by Ken Blanchard. A great book about management.

- *Make Better Decisions Under Pressure – Total Focus* (Mann 2017) by Brandon Webb and John David Mann. A sniper instructor turned entrepreneur's approach to improve situational awareness under stress.

- *Urban Survival Guide* (Morris 2013)[380], *Bartering and Negotiating in Post-Disaster Survival Situations*, by David Morris[381]. One of the most crucial time management ways to efficiently conduct results-oriented negotiation, bartering, and dickering.

- *The Unthinkable* (Ripley 2008, 2009)[382] by Amanda Ripley provides a deep examination of human response in a disaster and helps understand "who survives when a disaster strikes and why."

Resources oriented for emergency prepping

- A worthy book for emergency preparedness for rural or suburban communities is *The Civil Defense Book* (Mabee 2013, 2017, 2022)[383] by Michael Mabee.

- *One Second After* (Forstchen, One Second After 2009), *One Year After* (Forstchen, One Year After 2015), and *The Final Day* (Forstchen, The Final Day 2016) A trilogy of fiction books provide excellent insight into community and family survival in a post-EMP world. Very close to prophetic towards the unfolding times, a superb read for family and friends who haven't figured out the need for prepping yet.

- Excellent sources of prepping information from Claude Davis include *The Lost Ways* (Davis, The Lost Ways 2015), *The Lost Ways II* (Davis, The Lost Ways II 2019), *The Lost Super Foods* (Art Rude 2020), and the www.askaprepper.com[384] website. As Claude Writes, "I deeply believe the crisis we are all prepping for is what folks 150 years ago called daily life: no electricity, no refrigerators, no phones, no Internet, no gadgets, no pharmacies, no Walmart, and no effective law enforcement."

- *How To Survive the End Of The World As We Know It* (James Wesley 2009), by James Wesley, Rawles, founder of SurvivalBlog.com.

- *Where There Is No Doctor*[385], a village health care handbook, latest revision 2024. Werner, David. 2010. Berkeley, CA: Hesperian Foundation., (Werner 2010). The most widely used manual for health workers, educators, and others involved in primary care and health promotion worldwide. Every home should have a paper copy of an excellent medical care reference book, just in case.

- *Where There Is No Dentist*[386], an accompanying dental health care book, latest revision as of this writing) in 2010. Berkeley, CA: Hesperian Foundation., (Dickson 2010) Every home should have a paper copy of an excellent dental care reference book, just in case.

- *Nuclear War Survival Skills* (Kearney 1987)[387] by Cresson Kearny. Lifesaving nuclear facts and self-help instructions. A guide to stop-gap civil defense, which individuals now need to carry out for themselves as the American Government has decided to make virtually no effort to protect its citizens from the results of a nuclear attack.

Additional background information sources
- *Desk Ref* (Glover 1989-2011)[388] (and its counterpart *Pocket Ref*[389]) is your reference guide without Google and the Internet for data regarding air and gases, automotive, belts, pulleys and gears, carpentry and construction, chemistry and physics, computers, constants, drafting symbols, electrical, electronics, fasteners (anchors, bolts and threads, nails, spikes and staples), screws, first aid, and a lot of other general information. A homeschooling educator would be well served to consider using this book as a syllabus for building their children's common sense knowledge.

- *Tombstone, The Great Chinese Famine, 1958–1962* (Jisheng 2008), was written by Yang Jisheng in honor of his father, who was one of the millions killed by the mismanagement of Mao's totalitarian government. Yang Jisheng chose the book's title to give his father a lasting tombstone instead of a physical one, which a non-relative would likely repurpose. There was nothing natural about this natural disaster, and it serves as a warning as the U.S. slides toward the loss of the Constitutional Republic.

- A Christian perspective book, *Be Thou Prepared* (Gallups 2015), written by Carl Gallups, calls for prudent Christian preparation. The book is focused on the need for Christians to be prepared not only for their benefit but for the Kingdom's benefit as well. The wrongful arrest of New Orleans resident Zeitoun and his unjust imprisonment for 23 days after Katrina prompted the book.

- *Pulse Attack* (Furey 2022), written by Anthony Furey, shares the real story behind the secret weapon (development of an EMP weapon) that can destroy North America.

- *Comsec* (Justin Carroll 2019) is an excellent book written by former Marine Corps Special Operations Justin Carroll and former marine and Police Detective Drew M.[390], with a deep understanding of cellular phone issues and what to do to improve communications security.

CONCLUSION

[24] And let us consider how to stir up one another to love and good works, **25** not neglecting to meet together, as is the habit of some, but encouraging one another, and all the more as you see the Day drawing near. (Hebrews 10:24-25[391]). This book is written to help Christians enhance their emergency management skills.

Bible joke[392] courtesy of Melissa Tumino:
It seems there were these three professionals sitting around talking about the oldest profession.

- The doctor says, "Well, the Bible says that God took a rib out of Adam to make woman. Since that clearly required surgery, then the oldest profession is surely medicine."

- The engineer shakes his head and replies, "No, no. The Bible also says that God created the world out of void and chaos. To do that, God must surely have been an engineer. Therefore, engineering is the oldest profession."

- The politician smiles smugly and leans discreetly forward. "Ahh," he says, "but who do you think created the chaos?"

You may be interested in adding a spiritual survival kit[393] while completing your prepping logistics inventory to have something to leave behind for your loved ones who don't have Christ in their lives.

ABOUT THE AUTHOR

Roger Fraumann
roger@pbresilience.com
www.mtwtlod.com

Technology consultant providing analysis, business development, and related services.
ISC)2 CISSP, FCC GROLS/1c Commercial license, Extra Class Amateur Radio License,
MS Tech Ed, FBI InfraGard (EMP-NDRC SIG), USAF Veteran (TSgt, Hon.), Highest Clearance: DoD
TS-Crypto '70-'84

- ❖ 11+ Years United States Air Force
- ❖ 20+ Years IT companies including NCR, IBM, ISV's
- ❖ 12+ Years FEMA Major Disasters (Div Supervisor)

+ Disaster Management
+ Information System Security
+ International Business Relations
+ Technology and Ecosystem Analysis
+ Channel Development
+ Technical Writing
+ USAF Minuteman III G&C, SRAM ALCM electronics
+ USAF Technical Master Instructor

BIBLIOGRAPHY

Art Rude, Lex Rooker, Claude Davis, and Fred Dwight. 2020. *The Lost Super Foods.* Bannockburn, IL (from website): Global Brother SRL.

Blanchard, Ken. 2010. *Leading at a Higher Level.* Upper Saddle River, NJ: FT Press.

Davis, Claude. 2015. *The Lost Ways.* Bannockburn, IL (from website): (a Global Brother Production) extracted from Lost Ways II page 2.

—. 2019. *The Lost Ways II.* Bannockburn, IL (from website): (a Global Brother Production) extracted from Lost Ways II page 2.

Dickson, Murray. 2010. *Where There Is No Dentist.* Berkley, CA: Hesperian Foundation.

Federal Emergency Management Agency. 2020. *Are You Ready?* Washington, DC: Ready.gov.

Forstchen, William R. 2009. *One Second After.* New York, New York: Tom Doherty Associates, LLC.

—. 2015. *One Year After.* New York, New York: Tom Doherty Associates, LLC.

—. 2016. *The Final Day.* New York, New York: Tom Doherty Associates.

Furey, Anthony. 2022. *Pulse Attack.* Monee, IL: 20116 Magna Carta.

Gallups, Carl. 2015. *Be Thou Prepared.* Washington, DC: WND Books.

Glover, Thomas. 1989-2011. *Desk Ref.* Littleton, CO: Sequoia Publishing, Inc.

He, Jinliang. 2019. *Metal Oxide Varistors.* Boschstr. 1269469, Weinheim: Wiley-VCH Verlag GmbH &Co. KGaA.

Hunter, Nan D. 2018. *The Law of Emergencies, Public Health and Disaster Management, Second Edition.* Washington, District of Columbia: Butterworth-Heinemann.

James Wesley, Rawles. 2009. *How to survive the end of the world as we know it.* New York: PLUME Penguin Group.

Jisheng, Yang. 2008. *Tombstone, The Great Chinese Famine, 1958-1962.* New York, New York: Farrar, Straus and Giroux.

Justin Carroll, and Drew M. 2019. *COMSEC: Off-The-Grid Comm.* Middletown, DE.

Kearney, Cresson. 1987. *Nuclear War Survival Skills.* Cave Junction, OR: Oregon Institute of Science and Medicine.

Mabee, Michael. 2013, 2017, 2022. *The Civil Defense Book.* Monee, IL: Createspace independent publishing platform.

Mann, Brandon Webb, and John David. 2017. *Total Focus.* New York, New York: Penguin Random House LLC.

Merriam-Webster. 2024. *bug out.* 08 19. Accessed 08 19, 2024. https://www.merriam-webster.com/dictionary/bug out#h1.

Morris, David. 2013. *Urban Survival Guide.* Exeter, UK: CreateSpace Independent Publishing Platform, 2013.

Peterson, Dr. Jordan B. 2018. *12 Rules For Life, An Antidote To Chaos.* Toronto: Random House Canada.

Raz, Chris Voss with Tahl. 2016. *Never Split The Difference.* London: Random House Business.

Riley, Patrick Van Horne and Jason A. 2014. *Left of Bang.* New York, New York: Black Irish Entertainment LLC.

Ripley, Amanda. 2008, 2009. *The Unthinkable.* New York: Three Rivers Press.

Ross, Kirkham. 2023. *Poor Man's Bug Out Escape and Evasion.* Monee, IL.

Rummel, R. J. 1994. *Death By Government.* New Brunswick, New Jersey: Transaction Publishers.

Skousen, Joel M Skousen and Andrew. 2021 (Fourth Edition). *Strategic Relocation.* ISBN: 978-1-7350158-0-8.

U.S. Government Printing Office. 2024. *20XX Emergency Response Guidebook.* Washington DC: Superintendent of Documents, Government Printing Office.

Varozza, Georga. 2019. *The Homestead Canning Cookbook.* Eugene, OR: Ten Peaks Press.

Werner, David. 2010. *Where There Is No Doctor, a village health care handbook, Revised Edition.* Berkeley, CA: Hesperian.

Winks, David. 2020. *Protecting U.S. Electric Grid Communications From Electromagnetic Pulse.* Exeter, NH: Foundation For Resilient Societies.

INDEX

ENDNOTES

1 https://www.raptureready.com/2024/02/13/a-door-opened-in-heaven-rev-41-by-donald-whitchard/

2 https://www.forbes.com/sites/forbestechcouncil/2021/10/12/
why-disaster-recovery-is-no-longer-optional-for-todays-businesses

3 https://www.biblegateway.com/passage/?search=Ephesians%202%3A2&version=ESV

4 https://www.goodreads.com/quotes/8913100-in-any-moment-of-decision-the-best-thing-you-can

5 https://safetyculture.com/topics/emergency-management/

6 https://dictionary.cambridge.org/us/dictionary/english/emergency-responder/

7 https://www.droneresponders.org/

8 https://www.kenblanchardbooks.com/book/leading-at-a-higher-level/

9 https://www.merriam-webster.com/dictionary/bug%20out#h1, (Merriam-Webster 2024)

10 https://www.biblegateway.com/passage/?search=Isaiah%2045%3A7&version=ESV

11 https://www.biblegateway.com/passage/?search=Isaiah%2014%3A12-17&version=ESV

12 https://www.biblegateway.com/passage/?search=Galatians%205%3A22&version=ESV

13 https://www.gotquestions.org/order-vs-chaos.html

14 https://www.openbible.info/topics/chaos

15 https://thecontentauthority.com/blog/chaos-vs-havoc

16 https://www.biblegateway.com/passage/?search=Proverbs%209%3A10&version=ESV

17 https://www.biblegateway.com/passage/?search=Proverbs%202%3A6&version=ESV

18 https://www.nationalreview.com/2019/09/intentions-wisdom-and-evil/

19 http://www.vftonline.org/XianAnarch/pacifism/rummel.htm

20 https://archive.org/details/rummel-r.-j.-death-by-government-1994, (Rummel 1994)

21 https://www.verywellfit.com/daily-diet-composition-calculator-charts-carbs-protein-fat-3861072

22 https://www.psychologytoday.com/us/blog/living-eating-disorders/202108/
what-we-can-learn-the-minnesota-starvation-experiment

23 https://www.biblegateway.com/passage/?search=Romans%2013%3A1–7&version=ESV

24 https://www.forbes.com/sites/robertlenzner/2010/12/07/
soros-warns-us-could-be-on-verge-dictatorial-democracy-slams-fox-glen-beck/

25 https://www.biblegateway.com/passage/?search=Romans%2012%3A19-21&version=ESV

26 https://www.law.cornell.edu/wex/arbitrary

27 https://www.theatlantic.com/politics/archive/2011/05/
why-did-the-cdc-develop-a-plan-for-a-zombie-apocalypse/239246/

28 https://reason.com/volokh/2020/12/21/duty-to-retreat-35-states-vs-stand-your-ground-15-states/

29 https://press-pubs.uchicago.edu/founders/documents/amendIIs7.html

30 https://www.rasmussenreports.com/public_content/politics/current_events/gun_control/
gun_control_voters_say_enforcing_existing_laws_will_do_more_to_reduce_violence

31 https://www.rand.org/research/gun-policy/analysis/gun-free-zones.html

32 https://legaldictionary.net/duty-of-care/

33 https://iowafc.org/2015/09/09/10-years-ago-the-govt-went-door-to-door-
confiscating-guns-lets-keep-it-from-happening-again/

34 https://www.nbcnews.com/id/wbna27087738

35 https://washingtonmonthly.com/2016/03/15/hillary-clinton-barack-obama-and-saul-alinsky/

36 https://www.azquotes.com/quote/686713

37 https://www.azquotes.com/quote/686741

38 http://httpsfirescope.caloes.ca.gov/SiteCollectionDocuments/ICS History and Progress

39 https://training.fema.gov/emiweb/is/icsresource/assets/nims ics forms booklet.v3.pdf

40 https://sofrep.com/news/situational-awareness-a-navy-seal-explains/

41 https://www.nwcg.gov/committee/6mfs/operational-tempo

42 https://theodolite.app

43 https://brandontylerwebb.com/book/total-focus/

44 https://www.newsweek.com/craig-fugate-explains-waffle-house-index-1120655

45 https://www.spotonresponse.com/

46 https://www.convenience.org/

47 https://www.saberspace.org/

48 https://public.govdelivery.com/accounts/USDHSFEMA/subscriber/new

49 https://www.disastercenter.com

50 https://www.gdacs.org/gdacsregister

51 https://mwi.westpoint.edu/soldier-swarm-new-ground-combat-tactics-era-multi-domain-battle/

52 https://mwi.usma.edu/radios-jammed-fight-like-ants-swarms-soldiers-future-battlefield/

53 https://www.nwcg.gov/committee/6mfs/operational-tempo

54 https://www.refugemedical.com/

55 https://www.gps.gov

56 https://doi.org/10.6028/NIST.TN.2189

57 https://nvlpubs.nist.gov/nistpubs/TechnicalNotes/NIST.TN.2189.pdf

58 https://www.biblegateway.com/passage/?search=Amos%208%3A11&version=ESV

59 https://www.newscientist.com/definition/occams-razor/

60 https://www.forbes.com/sites/mikekappel/2021/09/15/keep-it-simple-stupid-applying-the-kiss-principle-to-reports-marketing--beyond/

61 https://www.businessinsider.com/guides/learning/never-split-the-difference-book-review?op=1

62 https://www.un.org/development/desa/disabilities/wp-content/uploads/sites/15/2020/03/Final-Disability-inclusive-disaster.pdf

63 https://georgewbush-whitehouse.archives.gov/reports/katrina-lessons-learned/chapter1.html

64 https://www.refugemedical.com/products/bearfak-individual-first-aid-kit?variant=45293095321816

65 https://jasemedical.com/case

66 https://www.redcross.org/take-a-class

67 https://www.ncbi.nlm.nih.gov/pmc/articles/PMC3273374/

68 https://www.crisis-medicine.com/march-versions/

69 https://www.redcross.org/volunteer/become-a-volunteer/urgent-need-for-volunteers.html

70 https://www.ready.gov/cert

71 https://training.fema.gov/emiweb/downloads/fog.pdf

72 https://archive.naplesnews.com/community/cert-team-nets-national-recognition-ep-406480030-332099082.html/

73 https://www.bainbridgeprepares.org/

74 http://FEMA-VAL@fema.dhs.gov

75 https://www.britannica.com/topic/broken-windows-theory

76 https://papers.ssrn.com/sol3/papers.cfm?abstract_id=2376272

77 https://www.americanthinker.com/articles/2019/07/the_lefts_endgame_is_not_chaos_its_worse.html

78 https://www.cfr.org/backgrounder/chinese-communist-party

79 https://historynewsnetwork.org/article/182642

80 https://www.bloomberg.com/news/articles/2019-11-05/scientists-call-for-population-control-in-mass-climate-alarm#xj4y7vzkg

81 https://www.hawaii.edu/powerkills/CHINA.CHAP1.HTM

82 https://www.oodaloop.com/documents/unrestricted.pdf

83 https://www.britannica.com/event/Holodomor

84 https://www.rand.org/pubs/perspectives/PE231.html

85 https://allthatsinteresting.com/pol-pot

86 https://www.ncbi.nlm.nih.gov/pmc/articles/PMC3612319/

87 https://slaynews.com/news/canadian-doctors-admit-covid-booster-shot-paralyzed-woman-offer-euthanize/

88 https://www.police1.com/police-trainers/articles/
coopers-colors-a-simple-system-for-situational-awareness-Np1Ni2TbRj9EkGUN/

89 https://www.unocha.org/story/five-essentials-first-72-hours-disaster-response

90 https://theprepared.com/prepping-basics/guides/bug-in-vs-bug-out/

91 https://salvationarmy.org/

92 https://www.redcross.org/

93 https://www.habitat.org/

94 https://duckduckgo.com/?q=Rubicon+emergency+response&ia=web

95 https://www.fema.gov/fact-sheet/disaster-recovery-centers

96 https://archive.org/details/unmaskingfacegui0000ekma

97 https://www.psychologytoday.com/us/blog/how-do-life/201404/how-can-you-tell-who-trust

98 https://orienteeringusa.org/explore/what-is-orienteering/

99 https://www.transportation.gov/pnt/what-positioning-navigation-and-timing-pnt

100 https://www.usni.org/magazines/proceedings/2022/july/surface-crews-need-more-tools-navigate-without-gps

101 https://www.time.gov/

102 https://www.nist.gov/pml/time-and-frequency-division/time-distribution/internet-time-service-its

103 https://www.popularmechanics.com/space/satellites/a5220/4343983/

104 https://gps-coordinates.org/

105 https://www.worldhistory.org/article/2197/harrisons-marine-chronometer/

106 https://link.springer.com/article/10.1007/s11277-020-07211-7

107 http://www.maptools.com/mgrs_history

108 https://earth-info.nga.mil/

109 https://www.fgdc.gov/usng/how-to-read-usng/index_html

110 https://www.chrono24.com/hamilton/ref-milw46374b.htm

111 https://wornandwound.com/military-watches-world-u-s-part-2/

112 https://www.omegawatches.com/en-us/watches/speedmaster/moonwatch-professional/product

113 https://www.techtarget.com/searchnetworking/definition/megahertz

114 https://www.nist.gov/pml/time-and-frequency-division/time-distribution/radio-station-wwv

115 https://en.wikipedia.org/wiki/WWVB

116 https://www.lacrossetechnology.com/products/404-1235ua-ss

117 https://www.iso.org/iso-8601-date-and-time-format.html

118 https://www.usgs.gov/tools/national-map-viewer

119 https://maptools.com/free_tools/utm_tools

120 https://store.randmcnally.com/rand-mcnally-2024-large-scale-road-atlas.html

121 https://www.usgs.gov/programs/national-cooperative-geologic-mapping-program/brief-history-geologic-mapping-usgs

122 https://nonprofitrisk.org/resources/e-news/put-on-your-thinking-map-create-a-contingency-map-in-5-steps/

123 https://www.hsdl.org/c/view?docid=749806

124 https://unitedstatesmaps.org/us-pipeline-map/

125 https://www.hsdl.org/c/abstract/?docid=12605

126 https://www.biblegateway.com/passage/?search=1%20John%202%3A26-29&version=ESV

127 https://www.army.mil/article/238308/situational_awareness_make_safe_choices

128 https://www.jjluna.com/

129 https://www.goodreads.com/book/show/8130304-urban-survival-guide

130 https://nnw.org/find-a-watch-program

131 https://www.nnw.org/

132 https://graywolfsurvival.com/3498/neighborhood-watch-just-nosey-old-ladies/

133 https://civildefensemanual.com/chapter-8-initial-steps-building-a-cdm-neighborhood-protection-plan/

134 https://www.sheriffs.org/about-nsa/history/roots

135 https://www.fema.gov/sites/default/files/2020-07/safe-rooms-design-criteria_recovery-advisory.pdf

136 https://www.fema.gov/emergency-managers/risk-management/building-science/safe-rooms

137 https://www.onallbands.com/emcomm-ham-radio-digital-modes-for-use-during-emergencies/

138 https://www.axis.com/files/feature_articles/ar_id_and_recognition_53836_en_1309_lo.pdf

139 https://pestcontroleverything.com/products/critter-pricker-raccoon-deterrent-proven-humane-dog-cat-garden-wall-defender-and-pest-control-10-connectable-spikes-on-strips

140 https://blockaides.com/blog/bollards-driveway-barriers-personal-use-homes/

141 https://urbansurvivalsite.com/best-plants-home-security/

142 https://foter.com/security-door-stop

143 https://doorarmor.com/

144 https://www.3m.com/3M/en_US/p/d/b5005059013/

145 https://www.lowes.com/n/how-to/how-to-install-garage-door-storm-braces

146 https://simplisafe.com/

147 https://www.adt.com/

148 https://urbansurvivalsite.com/diy-trip-wire-alarms/

149 https://www.kravmaga.com/

150 https://www.hxoutdoors.com/products/ft-12?_pos=3&_psq=axe&_ss=e&_v=1.0

151 https://graywolfsurvival.com/1179/how-to-family-emergency-communication-plan/

152 https://support.candlescience.com/hc/en-us/articles/201351324-How-do-I-calculate-the-burn-time-of-my-candles-

153 https://lookingforlights.com/how-long-does-an-oil-lamp-burn/?expand_article=1

154 https://deciwatt.global/shop/nl01

155 https://www.techpowerup.com/311525/how-to-size-your-solar-generator-for-running-a-refrigerator-a-comprehensive-guide-by-anker

156 https://commonsensehome.com/root-cellars-101/

157 https://tinylivinglife.com/5-best-off-grid-solar-refrigerators-in-2020/

158 https://www.reusablecanninglids.com

159 https://thehutchhouse.com/learn/dos-donts-water-bath-canning/

160 https://www.harvesthousepublishers.com/books/homestead-canning-cookbook-9780736978941

161 https://toolbox.igus.com/motion-plastics-blog/what-is-shore-power

162 https://www.health.ny.gov/publications/6594/

163 https://www.homedepot.com/s/ryobi bucket top misting fan?NCNI-5

164 https://www.treehugger.com/the-home-of-tomorrow-will-run-on-direct-current-4863157

165 https://www.redfin.com/blog/residential-microgrids-what-you-need-to-know-about-going-off-the-grid/

166 https://www.measuringknowhow.com/battery-sizes/

167 https://www.newscientist.com/article/2398896-what-are-solid-state-batteries-and-why-do-we-need-them/

168 https://www.cisco.com/c/en/us/solutions/enterprise-networks/what-is-power-over-ethernet.html

169 https://www.cablematters.com/Blog/Networking/cat6-vs-cat6a-vs-cat7

170 https://www.sciencedirect.com/science/article/abs/pii/S0142061521004944

171 https://www.esfi.org/workplace-safety/industry-codes-regulations/the-national-electrical-code-nec/

172 https://homeinspectioninsider.com/seismic-straps-on-water-heater/

173 https://www.freedrinkingwater.com/products/roes-phuv75-detail

174 https://www.govinfo.gov/content/pkg/FR-2019-03-27/pdf/2019-05770.pdf

175 https://www.popularmechanics.com/science/a33896110/tiny-nuclear-reactor-government-approval/

176 https://www.rpssolarpumps.com/get-sizing/

177 https://poweretty.com/blog/how-much-horsepower-do-you-need-for-a-pto-generator

178 https://simplepump.com/

179 https://www.watersourceusa.com/

180 https://www.sciencedirect.com/topics/earth-and-planetary-sciences/potable-water

181 https://science.howstuffworks.com/environmental/green-science/gray-water-reclamation1.htm

182 https://science.howstuffworks.com/environmental/green-science/gray-water-reclamation1.htm

183 https://gizmodo.com/could-you-drink-beer-instead-of-water-and-still-survive-457081579

184 https://www.platy.com/filtration/gravityworks-water-filter-system/gravityworks.html

185 https://www.northerntool.com/products/romotech-poly-storage-tank-square-50-gallon-capacity-model-2391-48169

186 https://www.seychelle.com/collections/radiological

187 https://miracle2ofutah.com/product/h2oresq-emergency-water-storage-treatment-kit/

188 https://offgridworld.com/how-to-make-a-5-gallon-bucket-water-filter/

189 https://www.epa.gov/sites/default/files/2015-04/documents/epa816f13002.pdf

190 https://www.openepanet.org/Topic/21619/20-psi

191 https://www2.deq.idaho.gov/admin/LEIA/api/document/download/4794

192 https://www.usgs.gov/special-topics/water-science-school/science/how-much-water-there-earth

193 https://solariswatergen.com/

194 https://www.israel21c.org/israeli-scientists-generate-water-from-air-even-in-the-desert/

195 https://www.nature.com/articles/s41586-021-03900-w

196 https://www.frontpagemag.com/
in-everything-to-do-with-water-israel-is-a-world-leader/?mc_cid=bee1d7658d&mc_eid=38bba96baa

197 https://www.prophecynewswatch.com/article.cfm?recent_news_id=6782

198 https://www.shamwow.com/

199 https://www.firstwaterinc.com/fw-120

200 https://www.rpssolarpumps.com/backup-water-systems

201 https://www.wef.org/globalassets/assets-wef/direct-download-library/public/03---resources/
wsec-2019-fs-013---csc-mrrdc---lift-stations-and-data-management---final.pdf

202 https://urbansurvivalsite.com/how-to-build-an-off-grid-bathroom/

203 https://homesteady.com/13425244/how-to-use-lime-in-an-outhouse

204 https://store.churchofjesuschrist.org/new-category/food-storage/food-storage/5637169327.c

205 https://heavensharvest.com

206 https://www.mypatriotsupply.com/

207 https://forgottensuperfoods.com/book/?aff_id=5855&subid=organic

208 https://oxygenabsorbers.com/oxygen-absorbers-scavengers-2000cc.html

209 https://www.generon.com/using-nitrogen-gas-in-food-packaging/

210 https://www.fda.gov/media/91319/download

211 https://www.energysage.com/energy-storage/islanding-and-batteries-what-you-need-to-know/

212 https://www.medeco.com/en

213 https://www.safewise.com/best-security-window-film/#Best_overall

214 https://www.galvinpower.org/best-automatic-transfer-switches/

215 https://readyforwildfire.org/prepare-for-wildfire/hardening-your-home/

216 https://www.fire.ca.gov/dspace

217 https://www.generac.com/

218 https://ftw.usatoday.com/2015/08/refuge-of-last-resort-five-days-inside-the-superdome-for-hurricane-katrina

219 https://joelskousen.com/strategic-relocation

220 https://definitions.uslegal.com/m/mandatory-evacuation/

221 https://www.cdc.gov/mmwr/volumes/69/wr/mm6936a1.htm

222 https://www.findlaw.com/legalblogs/criminal-defense/
can-you-be-arrested-for-not-complying-with-an-evacuation-order/

223 https://www.backdoorsurvival.com/three-unexpected-survival-tools-used-by-civil-war-soldiers/

224 https://ohsonline.com/Articles/2013/09/01/What-Is-a-Safe-Lift.aspx

225 https://www.spacepen.com/refills

226 https://www.fenixlighting.com/products/fenix-t6-penlight

227 http://www.swisstechtools.com/proddetail.aspx?PID=5

228 https://www.fenixlight.com/product/detail/index.php?id=47

229 https://www.leatherman.com/skeletool-18.html

230 https://www.inc.com/matt-given/this-1-lesson-from-how-the-navy-seals-plan-their-m.html

231 https://www.readyman.com/

232 https://www.readyman.com/collections/books/products/bug-out-comic

233 https://www.emergencyprepgear.com/72-hour-kit

234 https://www.firesupplydepot.com/cert-kits-supplies.html

235 https://www.stealthangelsurvival.com/collections/emergency-kits

236 https://herpackinglist.com/emergency-evacuation-packing-list/

237 https://modernsurvivalonline.com/get-out-of-dodge-bags/

238 https://www.skilledsurvival.com/inch-bag/

239 https://trueprepper.com/homeless-survival-kits/

240 https://www.reddit.com/r/pics/comments/gd3y84/been_working_on_a_shit_hit_the_fan_bag_since_i/

241 https://www.aarp.org/home-family/friends-family/info-2020/emergency-go-bag.html

242 https://www.primalsurvivor.net/trauma-kits/

243 https://www.ohscanada.com/overtime/flammable-materials-never-wear-job/

244 https://www.armyheritage.org/wp-content/uploads/ref-bibs/subjects/Marching/Marching%20Rates.pdf

245 https://www.law.cornell.edu/cfr/text/46/108.575

246 https://www.datrex.com/product-category/emergency-preparedness/survival-rations-and-water/

247 https://www.amazon.com/Emergency-Mylar-Thermal-Blankets-Pack/dp/B07C1J3P76

248 https://www.refugemedical.com/products/travel-fak

249 https://www.irwin.com/tools/locking-tools/5cr-vise-grip-multi-pliers

250 https://www.katadyngroup.com/us/en/item~p6775

251 https://www.nytimes.com/2024/07/09/us/copper-theft-heavy-metal.html

252 https://www.nytimes.com/wirecutter/reviews/best-duct-tape/

253 https://www.bobvila.com/articles/types-of-rope/

254 https://www.ucf.edu/online/leadership-management/news/the-disaster-management-cycle/

255 http://www.huffingtonpost.com/megan-devine/stages-of-grief_b_4414077.html

256 https://archive.hshsl.umaryland.edu/bitstream/handle/10713/15503/Explanation_
Emotional_Disaster_Slide-Rev%25206-23-21.pdf?sequence=5

257 https://www.thescienceofpsychotherapy.com/glossary/amygdala/

258 https://safestart.com/news/what-8020-rule-has-do-safety/

259 https://www.usni.org/magazines/naval-history-magazine/2010/december/70-miles-cold-hard-road

260 https://www.fema.gov/cbrn-tools/key-planning-factors-chemical-incident/appendix_f

261 https://www.fema.gov/about/offices/logistics

262 http://https/www.fema.gov/sites/default/files/2020-07/fema_ESF_7_Logistics

263 https://www.ready.gov/sites/default/files/2024-05/ready_supply-kit-checklist.pdf

264 https://www.ready.gov/kit

265 https://www.thebay.com/product/hbc-stripes-multistripe-point-blanket-0600001019439.html

266 https://www.nordisco.com/products/national-brand-56-231-record-book-300-pages-10-3-8-x-8-3-8.html

267 https://www.aaa.com/mapgallery/

268 https://www.loves.com

269 https://www.walmart.com/ip/ICE-MOUNTAIN-Brand-100-Natural-Spring-Water-
16-9-ounce-bottles-Pack-of-32/42678968?classType=REGULAR

270 https://www.walmart.com/ip/Charmin-Ultra-Soft-Toilet-Paper-18-Mega-XL-Rolls-336-Sheets-Per-Roll/1574894644

271 https://www.walmart.com/ip/Snickers-Full-Size-Chocolate-Candy-Bars-11-16-oz-6-Pack/33282383

272 https://www.walmart.com/ip/Newtons-Soft-Fruit-Chewy-Fig-Cookies-12-Snack-Packs-2-Cookies-Per-Pack/10292128

273 https://www.nordisco.com/products/scotch-810341296-3-4w-magic-tape.html

274 https://www.nordisco.com/products/uni-ball-207-retractable-gel-ubc33951.html

275 https://www.walmart.com/ip/Kidde-1-A-10-B-C-Full-Home-Fire-Extinguisher-2-5-Lb-14-7-16-x-4-5-8/748074755

276 https://www.walmart.com/search?q=1611559721,
Thrive-First-Aid-Kit-291-Piece-Supply-Hospital-Grade-Medical-Supplies

277 https://harbingersdaily.com/underground-bunkers-a-fulfillment-of-bible-prophecy/

278 https://prepperspriority.com/how-much-does-a-prepper-bunker-cost/

279 https://www.aei.org/articles/the-un-internet-takeover/

280 https://www.weather.gov/

281 https://midlandusa.com/product/er310-eready-emergency-crank-weather-radio/

282 https://ccrane.com/cc-skywave-ssb-2-with-am-fm-sw-wx-and-aviation-bands

283 https://etoncorp.com/products/elite-executive-radio

284 http://icomamerica.com/en/products/amateur/receivers/r30/default.aspx

285 https://ccrane.com/ssb-frequency-lists/

286 https://www.wiley.com/en-us/
Metal+Oxide+Varistors%3A+From+Microstructure+to+Macro+Characteristics-p-9783527684052

287 https://eiscouncil.org/black-sky/

288 https://www.arrl.org/files/file/Technology/tis/info/pdf/129756.pdf

289 https://www.arrl.org/learning-morse-code

290 https://www.arrl.org/digital-data-modes

291 https://www.arrl.org/files/file/Technology/tis/info/pdf/0003090a.pdf

292 https://www.walmart.com/ip/Motorola-Talkabout-T600-H2O-Waterproof-
FRS-Radios-walkie-talkies-22-Channel/50877955?from=/search

293 https://www.fcc.gov/wireless/bureau-divisions/mobility-division/citizens-band-radio-service-cbrs

294 https://uniden.com/products/bearcat-980

295 https://www.walcottradio.com/base-station-cb-antennas-c-377_352_632.html

296 https://www.dxengineering.com/parts/dxe-8xdx100

297 https://www.empshield.com/product/ant-200/

298 http://arrl.org/licensing-education-training

299 http://www.arrl.org/emergency-communications-training

300 https://www.arrl.org/files/file/Tech Band Chart/US Amateur Radio Technician Privileges.pdf

301 https://www.arrl.org/files/file/Education/ExtraClass/AC Waveforms and Measurements Review.pdf

302 https://www.findlaw.com/realestate/owning-a-home/what-is-a-common-interest-community.html

303 https://www.hopb.co/california-hoa-law-guide

304 https://theprepperjournal.com/2013/10/17/ham-radio-license-hide-government/

305 https://wireless2.fcc.gov/UlsApp/UlsSearch/searchAmateur.jsp

306 https://www.arrl.org/advanced-call-sign-search

307 https://www.qrz.com/lookup

308 https://www.radiomuseum.org/forum/radios_confiscated_in_us_during_wwii.html

309 http://findarticles.com/p/articles/mi_qn4196/is_19991219/ai_n10555142

310 https://cdn.rohde-schwarz.com/us/campaigns_2/a_d/Intro-to-direction-finding-methodologies~1.pdf

311 https://www.allaboutcircuits.com/technical-articles/introduction-to-software-defined-radio/

312 https://circuitcellar.com/insights/tech-the-future/advancements-in-dronerf-surveillance/

313 https://www.ncei.noaa.gov/access/billions/state-summary/US

314 https://chatgpt.com/share/f5497f9b-f6ec-4e67-9623-66b8913e2126

315 https://www.spaceweatherlive.com/en/help/what-is-a-coronal-mass-ejection-cme

316 http://www.empcommission.org/

317 https://eiscouncil.org/black-sky/

318 https://www.ncbi.nlm.nih.gov/books/NBK570437/

319 https://www.swpc.noaa.gov/phenomena/coronal-mass-ejections

320 https://www.astronomy.com/science/a-large-solar-storm-could-knock-out-the-internet-and-power-grid-an-electrical-engineer-explains-how/

321 https://www.space.com/the-carrington-event

322 https://www.eia.gov/electricity/gridmonitor/dashboard/electric_overview/US48/US48

323 https://www.gao.gov/blog/securing-u.s.-electricity-grid-cyberattacks

324 https://www.cfr.org/report/cyberattack-us-power-grid

325 https://www.eia.gov/todayinenergy/detail.php?id=27152

326 https://www.nrel.gov/grid/microgrids.html

327 https://www.energy.gov/ne/articles/nrc-certifies-first-us-small-modular-reactor-design

328 https://www.tesla.com/powerwall

329 https://www.generac.com/solar-battery-storage/pwrcell-product-overview/

330 https://bigbattery.com/products/24kw-40-9kwh-ethos-energy-storage-system-ess/

331 https://www.victronenergy.com

332 https://dakotalithium.com/product/dakota-lithium-home-backup-power-energy-storage-system-5-20-kwh-battery-3000-watt-inverter/

333 https://www.techtarget.com/searchstorage/definition/WORM-write-once-read-many

334 https://www.gao.gov/products/gao-23-106717

335 https://www.bbc.com/news/world-us-canada-55203844

336 https://www.themarysue.com/leave-the-world-behind-controversy-explained/

337 https://edition.cnn.com/2018/06/22/politics/pacific-ocean-us-military-jets-lasers-intl/index.html

338 https://science.howstuffworks.com/e-bomb3.htm

339 https://spectrum.ieee.org/ebombs-what-is-the-threat

340 https://www.futurescience.com/emp/E1-E2-E3.html

341 http://www.firstempcommission.org/uploads/1/1/9/5/119571849/recommended_e3_waveform_for_critical_infrastructures_-_final_april2018.pdf

342 https://www.cisa.gov/sites/default/files/publications/19_0307_CISA_EMP-Protection-Resilience-Guidelines.pdf

343 https://www.energy.gov/sites/prod/files/2017/01/f34/DOE%20EMP%20Resilience%20Action%20Plan%20January%202017.pdf

344 https://wiki.ezvid.com/best-faraday-bags-for-phones

345 https://www.empshield.com/

346 https://disasterpreparer.com/product/emp-alert/

347 https://www.nbcbayarea.com/news/local/equipment-stolen-from-metcalf-substation-site-of-2013-sniper-attack-san-jose-april/80327/

348 https://money.cnn.com/2015/10/16/technology/sniper-power-grid/index.html

349 https://spectrum.ieee.org/attack-on-nine-substations-could-take-down-us-grid

350 https://www.cisa.gov/resources-tools/services/wireless-priority-service-wps

351 https://www.cisa.gov/resources-tools/services/government-emergency-telecommunications-service-gets

352 https://www.cisa.gov/sites/default/files/publications/LMR%20101_508FINAL_0_0.pdf

353 https://www.firstnet.com

354 https://www.britannica.com/event/Tokyo-subway-attack-of-1995

355 https://www.bbc.com/news/world-middle-east-23927399s

356 https://archives.nato.int/uploads/r/nato-archives-online/e/1/4/
e14709e259e774cad586f7fe81b84f374b87e829cd917811c19b39791ae4b3fe/1267_
Guidelines-for-first-responders-CBRN_2007_ENG.pdf

357 https://www.weather.gov/pqr/wind

358 https://www.calculatorsoup.com/calculators/math/speed-distance-time-calculator.php

359 https://windsockusa.com

360 https://www.nature.com/articles/d41586-023-03509-1

361 https://www.opcw.org/about-us/member-states

362 https://www.healthline.com/health/bleach-and-ammonia#what-to-do-if-exposed

363 https://www.verywellhealth.com/mixing-bleach-and-ammonia-1298711

364 https://teamrubiconusa.org/news-and-stories/how-to-clean-up-after-a-flood/

365 https://www.nae.edu/19579/19582/21020/7392/7623/ToxicandContaminantConcernsGeneratedbyHurricaneKatrina

366 https://www.phmsa.dot.gov/news/usdot-announces-publication-2024-emergency-response-guidebook

367 https://www.phmsa.dot.gov/sites/phmsa.dot.gov/files/2024-04/ERG2024-Eng-Web-a.pdf

368 https://www.sciencedirect.com/book/9780128042755/the-law-of-emergencies

369 https://www.latimes.com/archives/la-xpm-2001-oct-14-mn-57096-story.html

370 https://health.clevelandclinic.org/crispr-gene-editing

371 https://www.nbcnews.com/health/health-news/cdc-fungal-infection-candida-auris-alarming-spread-rcna75477

372 https://my.clevelandclinic.org/health/diseases/24862-black-mold

373 https://www.fema.gov/sites/default/files/documents/fema_cleaning-flooded-buildings-hurricane-sandy-fs-001.pdf

374 https://www.thelancet.com/journals/lancet/article/PIIS0140-6736(16)00144-6/abstract

375 http://nukalert.com

376 https://www.biblegateway.com/passage/?search=Genesis+1

377 https://www.biblegateway.com/passage/?search=Revelation+1

378 https://www.britannica.com/science/chaos-theory

379 https://www.biblegateway.com/passage/?search=John%208%3A44&version=ESV

380 https://www.abebooks.com/servlet/BookDetailsPL?bi=17095227695

381 https://surviveinplace.com

382 https://www.amandaripley.com/the-unthinkable

383 https://michaelmabee.info/civil-defense-book-second-edition-available/

384 http://www.askaprepper.com

385 https://store.hesperian.org/prod/Where_There_Is_No_Doctor.html

386 https://store.hesperian.org/prod/Where_There_Is_No_Dentist.html

387 https://www.oism.org/nwss/

388 https://sequoiapublishing.com/product/desk-ref/

389 https://sequoiapublishing.com/product/pocket-ref/

390 You can look up "Hiding From The Internet", but be careful of being "Watchdogged"

391 https://www.biblegateway.com/passage/?search=Hebrews%2010%3A24-25&version=ESV

392 https://thinkaboutsuchthings.com/bible-jokes/

393 http://www.prophecydepotministries.net/?wref=bif

Made in the USA
Monee, IL
03 December 2024